MINISTRY LESSONS

Wisdom for Pastors from Pastors

GREG BURDINE

COPYRIGHT

Ministry Lessons: Widom for Pastors from Pastors

Copyright 2019 by Greg Burdine

ISBN-13: 9781688698987

DEDICATION

This book is dedicated to my pastors. Most of them have already finished their life journey and have received their reward for faithful service. A few are in retirement. But every one of them has left a permanent mark on my life. I am eternally grateful for the lessons each of them has taught me.

Nolan Phillips — University Baptist Church in Middletown, OH

Joe Lewis & Marty Lewis — Trinity Baptist Temple in Middletown, OH

Larry Lilly & Lee Singley (youth pastors) — Trinity Baptist Temple in Middletown, OH

David Cavin — High Street Baptist Church in Springfield, MO

Bill Dowell — Baptist Temple in Springfield, MO

Bill Taylor & Ival Robinson — Bible Baptist Church in Ottumwa, IA

Bill Dinoff — Fellowship Baptist Church in Columbus, OH

CONTENTS

PREFACE

"They didn't teach me that in Bible college!"

I loved my experience in Bible College. Some of my closest friends are those I met at Baptist Bible College. I also had great professors who instilled a love for God and a thorough understanding of doctrine and theology. Yet, it was only a few weeks after graduation and into my first position as a youth pastor that I realized there were more lessons to learn.

My first pastor boss, Bill Taylor, shared many practical lessons he had learned in his years of ministry. Most had to do with relationships with church members. Others had to do with personal issues. I remember one situation when he had to deal with divorce and remarriage within the church. He wasn't sure what he should do, but encouraged me to watch and learn.

In ministry life, many lessons are learned from other pastors. When I thought about writing this book, I knew I needed some help. I have learned many practical lessons about ministry. But with the help of some of my pastor friends, I now have a whole book of practical lessons about ministry. I simply asked each of them to share the one lesson they would like to share with other pastors.

This book is designed to share valuable time-tested lessons from men who have pastored for many, many years. Most of these men have pastored the same church for over a quarter of a century. If you added them all up, there are over 200 years of ministry experience in this book. I want to thank each of the pastors who made a contribution to this book. Your friendship is a blessing to me and hope your chapter will be a blessing to other pastors.

My prayer is that these lessons will save a young pastor from making some of the same mistakes these experienced pastors have made. I am also hoping that these lessons will give some guidance and wise counsel to a discouraged pastor who does not know what to do in a church mess. If you are not a pastor, I hope you will begin to understand the complicated situations in which pastors often find themselves.

This is not an exhaustive list of ministry lessons. If you are a pastor and have learned other lessons besides those mentioned in this book, please let me know. I may need to have a second edition.

God Bless You,

Greg Burdine

www.gregburdine.com

Spend Time Every Day With God

Greg Burdine

*"And in the morning, rising up a great while before day,
he went out, and departed into a solitary place, and
there prayed." (Mark 1:35)*

MORNINGS HAVE ALWAYS been a challenge for me. I am not a morning person. At least, at the beginning of my ministry, I would get out of bed at the last minute to shower, no breakfast, and out the door to my first appointment. I didn't "wake up" until about mid-morning and consume a candy bar and Pepsi for my late breakfast. No time to prepare myself for the day. No time to spend time with God. Barely enough time to get everything done that needed to be completed. I felt important because I felt busy.

But that all came crashing down when my son was shot in 2006 while serving in the Marines in Iraq. We received the call and it turned our world upside down. He nearly died from the blood loss. However, he recovered and had a month of rehabilitation at Bethesda Naval Hospital. I went out and spent the whole month with him. It's a month that has defined who I am as a father and a Christian.

I am very familiar with hospitals. As a pastor, I spend quite a bit of time visiting people in the hospital. But I wasn't visiting for a few minutes nor was I a patient. For many, many days, I had all day looking for something to do. So I picked up a Bible and started reading it.

I've read the Bible through a couple of times in my life. But this time I read the whole Bible in less than a month. I even started reading it the second time before the time came to go home. I left that Bible behind, but when I got home I picked up where I left off with my preaching Bible. Even with my busy schedule, I discovered that I had to carve out time to read my Bible. I had created a thirst for God's Word that nothing else in my schedule could quench.

That is when I started getting up early to read my Bible. I also discovered that early morning is the best time of the day. It is quiet. The craziness of my schedule and the crazies that I sometimes interact with aren't filling my mind with more crazy. It is just me and God. It is beautiful. It is productive.

When I get up in the morning and make time for God, I am guaranteeing that my most important priority is getting done. Nothing else I do all day will compare in value with my time with God. So, even if I get nothing else accomplished, I got my Number One Priority completed.

What is Quiet Time?

Christians down through the centuries have set aside a small portion of each day to shut out the world and focus on building their relationship with God. This time has been called many things: Quiet Time, Daily Devotions, The Morning Watch, Time Alone With God. I have always favored the term "Quiet Time." Your Quiet Time is when you get alone with God for the purpose of fellowship and worship. Those who have made their Quiet Time a priority in their lives point to it as one of the main keys to depth in their walk with God.

"The amount of time we spend with Jesus, meditating on His Word and His majesty, seeking His face, establishes our fruitfulness in the kingdom."

— Charles Stanley

"Ten minutes spent in the presence of Christ every day, aye, two minutes, will make the whole day different."

— Henry Drummond

"We are too busy to pray, and so we are too busy to have power. We have a great deal of activity, but we accomplish little; many services but few conversions; much machinery but few results."

— R. A. Torrey

"Time spent alone with God is not wasted. It changes us; it changes our surroundings; and every Christian who would live the life that counts, and who would have power for service must take time to pray."

— M. E. Andross

"If we don't maintain a quiet time each day, it's not really because we are too busy; it's because we do not feel it is important enough."

— George Sweeting

"Don't pray when you feel like it. Have an appointment with the Lord and keep it. A man is powerful on his knees."

— Corrie ten Boom

Notice how Jesus had His quiet time. *"And in the morning, rising up a great while before day, he went out, and departed into a solitary place, and there prayed." (Mark 1:35)*

Following a busy day and before another day began, He got up early to spend quiet time with His Heavenly Father. Late hours did not keep Jesus from His appointed meeting with His Father early in the morning. He knew that if He was to meet men he must first meet God.

As brief as it is, this picture of Jesus at quiet time is very instructive. He found a solitary place and prayed. Every person has some measure of power. We control our schedule and decide our priorities. No matter how busy you are, you make time for your priorities. The fundamental issue is not how we can cram more into our busy lives, but how we use what time we have. In this sense, we might even speak of our Quiet Time as a barometer of faith. If we do not have a Quiet Time, it is quite possible that we are operating on our own agenda and have refused our proper role as ministers.

All Christians need time alone with God. It is vital. But ministers, especially, need to spend time with God. We are examples of what a Christian should do. We are leaders and if we don't get it right, we will lead a whole congregation down the wrong path. Personally, we need fellowship with God. We were created to have fellowship with God; Jesus died so that we could have fellowship. To miss our Quiet Time is to miss our most important appointment of the day.

"If you want to find out what a man is really like, find out what he is like alone with God"

What Is Involved in Having a Quiet Time?

I am glad God doesn't make a list of expectations for our Quiet Time. It may vary from person to person. However, there are some simple principles that would help you have a regular, consistent Quiet Time.

1. **Set aside a particular time to spend alone with God.**

   It must be predetermined. If you don't set aside a time, you won't have the time. Jesus predetermined the time. Jesus did so before the day began. It must be planned. How much time will you spend? Notice that Jesus planned to spend a good amount of time. He went "a great while before day." It needs to be unhurried.

2. **Set aside a particular place to get alone with God.**

   It needs to be a place where you can be quiet and un-interrupted. Notice Jesus went to a "solitary place." This is important if you are to unclutter your mind so you can meet with God. The psalmist quotes our Heavenly Father when He said: *"be still, and know that I am God" (Ps 46:10).*

3. **Take God's Word with you to your time alone with God.**

God's Word (the Bible) is the primary tool that God uses to speak to us. Lately, I am reading less, not more. It's not a contest anymore to see how much I can read my Bible. I am reading one or two chapters, finding a verse that hits my heart, and making some observations and personal application. The goal is not just to read the Bible (though that is important), but to let the Bible read you. Slow down and listen.

4. **Spend time in prayer, talking heart to heart with God.**

Pray with purpose and direction. Just having a conversation with God is wonderful. However, it is also valuable to have some structure. Many Christians use acronyms to guide them: For example, A.C.T.S. (Adoration, Confession, Thanksgiving, Supplication) or P.R.A.Y. (Praise, Repent, Ask, Yield). I have often simply used the Lord's Prayer as my guide. Currently, I am using the example of twelve points of prayer from Dick Eastman's book, *The Hour That Changes the World.*

Regardless of what method you use to aid you in your prayer, make sure there is a time when you sit quietly and listen to the voice of God. We must be still so we can hear his voice. He will comfort you during this time. He will direct you to scripture during this time. He will direct your spirit during this time.

What Are the Benefits of Having a Quiet Time?

1 – Peace. Through refocusing your attention on God, rather than your problems, you will discover the promised peace of God. Life has a way of making our problems look bigger and our God look smaller. Your Quiet Time will readjust your perspective. *"And the peace of God, which passeth all understanding, shall keep your hearts and minds through Christ Jesus" (Philippians 4:7).*

2 – Joy. Because the source of your strength becomes Christ rather than your circumstances, you will maintain joy in spite of your circumstances. The ministry always has moments that cause pain and hurt. Don't let the ministry rob you of the joy of the presence of Jesus. *"Thou wilt shew me the path of life: in thy presence is fulness of joy; at thy right hand [there are] pleasures for evermore." (Psalm 16:11).*

3 – Direction. Spending time with God enables Him to give you direction when you need it. Even if you do not receive specific direction, God will bless the path you take as you acknowledge him in your decision. *"In all thy ways acknowledge him and he shall direct thy paths." (Prov. 3:5-6).* Notice that God does not necessarily direct our steps, but He will direct whatever path we take.

4 – Power/Strength. The ministry can be exhausting. It is an impossible task for our simple human strength. We need supernatural power and that only comes by waiting on God. *"But they that wait upon the LORD shall renew their strength; they shall mount up with wings as eagles; they shall run, and not be weary; and they shall walk, and not faint." (Isaiah 40:31)*

5 – Success. Joshua received a great promise from God that can apply to our ministry. *"This book of the law shall not depart out of thy mouth; but thou shalt meditate therein day and night, that thou mayest observe to do according to all that is written therein: for then thou shalt make thy way prosperous, and then thou shalt have good success." (Joshua 1:8)*. Joshua was a great success as a military leader. We can be a great success in our ministry by daily meditating on God's Word. Success is not found in buildings and budgets, but in hearing *"Well done, good and faithful servant" (Matthew 25:21)*.

6 – Others will notice the difference in our lives. Your Quiet Time is the foundation of a good ministry. If it is done right, no one will know the quantity and quality of your time with God. It is easy to cut corners in our Quiet Time. No one will know. But God will know. In regards to our private worship, Jesus promised: *"thy Father which seeth in secret shall reward thee openly" (Matthew 6:6)*. People may not know how or why, but they will know we have been with Jesus. *"Now when they saw the boldness of Peter and John, and perceived that they were unlearned and ignorant men, they marvelled; and they took knowledge of them, that they had been with Jesus." (Acts 4:13)*

There are many problems that we face when we try to maintain a Quiet Time. It may be discipline (consistent daily), boredom (dry), concentration, and even discouragement. The main thing to remember is to always pray and ask the Lord to help you.

Then commit yourself to just doing it. If you miss then do it the next day. Don't be committed to the schedule but the purpose.

It is said that Andrew Bonar, a great man of prayer, had three rules:

1. Not to speak to any man before speaking to Jesus.

2. Not to do anything with his hands until he had been on his knees.

3. Not to read the papers until he had read his Bible.

A missionary in Africa mentions a phenomenon that occurred as Christianity began to spread among some natives. In the early part of the day, as the men went to work, they would wander through the tall grass and find a quiet place to spend time with God. Soon the worn down grass became a dirt path that marked each one's journey to have a Quiet Time. Soon, one's prayer life was made public. If someone began to neglect his or her devotional life, it would soon be noticed by others. Believers would then gently and lovingly remind those in neglect, *'The grass grows on your path.''*

If you are too busy to spend time with God, you are busier than He intended you to be.

DISCOVER THE SWEET-SPOT OF FAITH AND WORKS

Tim Adrian

"Thus says the Lord: "Let not the wise man glory in his wisdom, Let not the mighty man glory in his might, nor let the rich man glory in his riches; But let him who glories glory in this, That he understands and knows Me, That I am the Lord, exercising lovingkindness, judgment, and righteousness in the earth, For in these I delight," says the Lord." (Jeremiah 9:23-24)

I WAS EXCITED to attend Bible College in the Los Angeles area. Sunny weather, the beach, Disneyland, Hollywood, nearby mountains, and of course California girls had all piqued my interest. I had a couple of real close buddies coming to school with me and we anticipated a year filled with a lot of laughter, a lot of adventure, and oh yeah, a bit of study. My dorm consisted of about twenty-five guys and nearly all of us were young teenaged freshmen. It was quickly evident all of us would need part-time jobs and that became the number one request at our weekly dorm prayer meetings.

Within three or four weeks, almost all of us had secured employment except two guys down the hall. I think everybody in the dorm took turns approaching these guys and passing along tips about potential jobs and the names of places accepting applications. Several more weeks passed and then we discovered the unique strategy of these two unemployed dorm-mates. It seems every afternoon, following a brief prayer that petitioned God to give them jobs, they retired to their bunks for a "season of rest." Is it a surprise they remained unemployed? Perhaps we all learned God is inclined to answer the prayers of people who actually work alongside Him.

Your grandma was right when she said: "God helps those who help themselves" and even though it's not Scripture verbatim, the principle is easy to find in the Bible. I like to think there is an intersection where our human effort meets our total reliance on God. It's the sweet-spot that results in God's best blessings. I used to hear Jerry Falwell say, "Work like everything depends on you and pray like everything depends on God." I had an old Sunday School teacher put it this way, "Boys, put feet to your prayers."

Just a few years after college, I'm married with three small kids, and God called us to plant a church in Arizona. We had enjoyed youth ministry in two wonderful churches and truly believed we were ready to step out this way. We were still in our twenties so we were probably long on energy and short on knowledge. Pam and I were genuinely excited about the venture, but we were basically clueless. This was before the formation and publication of church planting assessments, strategies, workbooks, and mentors so we did what we knew; pray hard and work hard. It now seems utterly ludicrous... we unloaded the U-Haul truck in the middle of a Phoenix summer and held our first services four weeks later with 23 in attendance. It seems unbelievable to me now, but six families joined us that first Sunday and all six attended for at least the first five years of the church's history.

After our church plant launch, people joined with us and our growth was steady albeit somewhat slow. It was a thrill to see people saved and baptized and soon we were able to give to missionary causes. I'm quite certain we were very typical in that our financial growth lagged somewhat behind our numerical growth.

We had raised some financial support, but at the time many churches were accustomed to giving help for only about 12 months. When possible, I worked part-time but financial concerns were always present. It seemed God regularly surprised us with unexpected gifts and frankly we learned one faith lesson after another in ways I can hardly describe.

We were about two years into the church plant when our offerings hit a level that I had been praying for. Not only did our folks begin to give at a higher level, but new families came our way that had already understood the grace of giving. I was probably a bit too proud when I called the last of our supporters and announced we no longer needed their help. In short order, God had a way to scrape some of the arrogance right off me.

One Saturday, I fielded two separate phone calls within 15 minutes of each other. They were from the two largest donors in our baby church. Both were being transferred out of state and both would obviously take their offerings with them. I was devastated as I suddenly knew we were in real trouble. My dreams of buying property for the church were replaced by the nightmare of knowing I would probably have to take a major pay cut.

Late that Saturday afternoon, I found myself at the rented day-care center where we held our services. I typically spent an hour or so making sure everything was clean and ready for the next day. Burdened and probably fearful about our future, I remember running the vacuum with tears running down my cheeks. It was during those few minutes God and I had a conversation. I ended up asking myself some serious questions and then came to some equally serious conclusions.

Had I really taken the credit for God's blessings? Had I really minimized God's part in our success? Was I willing to admit that, as our offerings went up, my acknowledgement of God went down? I felt like I was guilty of working for God but became somewhat independent from Him.

God had me in a ministry crisis. Losing two prominent families showed me just how vulnerable our baby church was before God. More importantly, He was showing me just how vulnerable I was. Being reliant on Him was a place I needed to be in, and a place where I needed to stay.

The afternoon nappers back in my college dorm prayed regularly but didn't work. Now I was guilty of the more egregious opposite. I had slipped into a habit of working without much prayer. God always has a way of getting the attention of His students and then implementing His custom-designed curriculum. In the day-care, He began to teach me several valuable lessons.

Ministry Crisis Clarifies Spiritual Issues

First of all, I realized my ministry crisis helped to bring clarity to certain spiritual issues. The drift towards "selfism" was gradual but certain. It is haunting to admit, but my attitude and behavior would have never changed if it were not for the crisis. It was the crisis that pinpointed my need and challenged my heart. It was the crisis that motivated my desire to listen to God behind the vacuum cleaner. It took a ministry crisis to bring about growth in my spiritual and personal life and, sadly, I just don't think it would have happened any other way.

Ministry Crisis Magnifies Spiritual Impotence

Secondly, the crisis magnified my own spiritual impotence. In the midst of all this, I was teaching and preaching and witnessing. God was honoring our faithfulness but it became evident I wasn't hitting the sweet spot. It was as if God were saying, "I can add to your church, but remember I can take them away too." God made it clear, He wanted me to enjoy a higher level of fruitfulness but revival needed to happen first. I didn't want to just spin my wheels. I wanted to be used by God for great things and that just wasn't going to happen if I didn't realign my heart.

Ministry Crisis Tests Commitment and Resolve

Additionally, I think God was testing my commitment and re-solve. Pam and I had left a wonderful situation and church fam-ily in Kansas City before we relocated to start the church. Now that we were facing a bit of discouragement, would we be just as committed? Behind the vacuum, I sensed God wanted me to say "yes" to Him again. It is at these times we should remember the call of God and possibly even rehearse past blessings. So, much like David recalled killing the lion and the bear before facing Goliath, I acknowledged my willingness to start the deliberate walk back onto the battlefield. Looking back, I am so grateful I said "yes" to God again that day.

Ministry Crisis Develops Faith Maturity

The ministry crisis also added another lesson in the develop-ment of my quest toward faith maturity. I had willingly put my eternal soul into God's hand and time and again had been called to place my earthly future into His control as well. This test would revolve around financial uncertainty and it brought me to a place where I had to determine where I stood. Would I rest in His promises or would I react with worry, anxiety and possibly anger? And how would I respond to our small congregation of seventy people? Would I be a man of faith or not? God was challenging me.

Ministry Crisis Magnifies God's Answer and Blessing

Finally, the ministry crisis would magnify God's eventual answer and blessing. God had driven me to my knees on Saturday, but the very next day He assured me and our entire church of a great future. For the first two years of our church, almost every single family that attended had received a personal invitation from our family. Some were cold calls and some were leads that we followed up but we could point to the path that brought everyone to our church. The Sunday after my vacuum cleaner revival saw four different families walk in through the door that we did not know or invite. Our church ministry stayed right on course, as eventually all four families became quite involved and generous givers to the ministry. God has rarely answered my crisis questions so completely and so quickly as He did that weekend. But it was obviously a tremendous lesson and something I've looked back to frequently.

*** *** ***

Years have passed since my time behind the vacuum. My ministry seems more complicated now. I've endured building programs, seen staff members come and go, and have had times of abundance and times that were very lean. At the end of each day, I still need to recognize the unique partnership I have with God. He has asked me to "present my body as a living sacrifice" and He has promised to "open the windows of heaven and pour out incredible blessings." It is my challenge to take care of my side of this arrangement and then patiently wait on God to bless as He sees fit and in the way He sees fit.

Baseball hitters talk about the sweet spot. Hitting a ball there typically results in line drives or even a home run. Just a tick off of that spot brings about weak pop-ups or slow grounders resulting in just another out. The sweet spot of ministry is that place where we are working hard and smart, yet remain reliant upon God for the outcomes. Isn't it exhilarating when we connect with God at the sweet spot?

My prayer continues: Lord keep me passionate; I need to work with enthusiasm and lots of energy. Lord keep me focused; I want to work the right way on the right things. Lord keep me humble; I don't ever want to deflect glory from You.

Tim Adrian has been the Lead Pastor at Westside Baptist Church in Hutchinson, Kansas for over 22 years. Under his ministry, Westside has sent eleven families to the mission field. His past ministries include starting churches in Colorado and Arizona. He earned his BA degree from Liberty University, and graduate degrees from Louisiana Baptist University. Tim is the current President of Baptist Bible Fellowship International (2019)..

Go Back to Your Base

Gary Fuller

I NEVER THOUGHT I would get one, but I did! You know those robotic vacuum cleaners that provide great entertainment for the pets? Turns out they are mildly enthralling for distracted pastors too. Our church families take turns cleaning up the church and the most time-consuming chore is the vacuuming. So, we purchased one for the church families as an Easter gift.

The thing that surprised me most is, they actually work! I was impressed at how much debris was collected and how fresh the floors looked and felt after it had bounced off of about a thousand pew chair legs, meandering around the building in no particular fashion. The little machine reminds me of a topical preacher meandering around the Scripture, covering the Bible in the most inefficient way possible, but he eventually gets the job done and was very entertaining in the interim.

The most impressive thing that little round robot did, in my way of thinking, was when its battery began to run down, it intuitively sought out its base, docked itself and received a fresh charge so it could go out and do its thing again the next time.

Ministry is a draining vocation. Ministers of the gospel are never off the clock. We do as much or more ministry away from the pulpit and the office as in them. Our minds are consumed constantly with building our churches, developing programs, restoring relationships, creating messages and lessons, meeting budgets, caring for souls, resolving staffing issues, stewarding properties, tending civic responsibilities and bolstering our own spirituality. The 24/7/365 nature of ministry often punches our tickets for emotional, mental, physical and spiritual roller coaster rides with more corkscrews, loop-d-loops, plunges and climbs than we ever could imagine.

The quadfecta of fatigue we suffer (emotional, mental, physical and spiritual) is compounded by unrealistic expectations. The nature of our gig is that we are subjected to living in a fish bowl. Transparency is expected and demanded from within and without. Congregants can't help but mentally monitor what we spend, where we travel, what hours we keep, when we fail, how we dress, what car we drive, how many toys we own, what our wives and daughters wear, the length of our sermons, the graying of our hair, or the lack of it, the number of hands we shake (or don't), our punctuality, our level of sacrifice, our income and our ability to tell a joke with dead on timing.

Most of what they imagine about these things are their perceptions, not the reality; their preferences, not our liberty. Therefore, we find ourselves catering to perceptions, what people might think, and preferences, what they want and expect, and we perform accordingly. That's not ministry, that's insanity. Additionally, there is the enormous pressure we impose upon ourselves. Ministry isn't for wimps, is it?

Of course, I have intentionally left out the greatest aspect of ministry until now, that feature is our relationship with Christ, our acceptance in the Beloved, our supernatural energy garnered from our Heavenly resources. And that brings me back to our little wandering robot. When the batteries begin to discharge, it intuitively knows when to head for its base for a recharge.

Ministers, are we docking in our charger often enough? Do we return regularly to our base to unplug from the work and plug into the power?

Some Saddening Statistics

I want to give you some very sobering numbers. They come from a newly revised update by Pastoral Care Inc.

- 72% of pastors report working between 55 to 75 hours per week.

- 84% of pastors feel they are on call 24/7.

- 80% believe pastoral ministry has negatively affected their families. Many pastor's children do not attend church now because of what the church has done to their parents.

- 65% of pastors feel their family lives in a "glass house" and fear they are not good enough to meet expectations.

- 78% of pastors report having their vacation and personal time interrupted with ministry duties or expectations.

- 65% of pastors feel they have not taken enough vacation time with their family over the last 5 years.

- 66% of church members expect a minister and family to live at a higher moral standard than themselves.

- 53% of pastors report that the seminary did not prepare them for the ministry.

- 90% of pastors report the ministry was completely different than what they thought it would be like before they entered the ministry.

- 95% of pastors report not praying daily or regularly with their spouse.

- 57% of pastors believe they do not receive a livable wage.

- 57% of pastors report being unable to pay their bills.

- 53% of pastors are concerned about their future family financial security.

- 80% of pastors and 84% of their spouses have felt unqualified for and discouraged in their role as pastors at least one or more times in their ministry.

- 52% of pastors feel overworked and cannot meet their church's unrealistic expectations.

- 54% of pastors find the role of a pastor overwhelming.

- 80% of pastors expect conflict within their church.

- 75% of pastors report spending 4-5 hours a week in needless meetings.

- 35% of pastors battle depression or fear of inadequacy.

- 26% of pastors report being overly fatigued.

- 28% of pastors report they are spiritually undernourished.

- 70% of pastors report they have a lower self-image now than when they first started.

- 70% of pastors do not have someone they consider to be a close friend.

- 81% of pastors have been tempted to have inappropriate sexual thoughts or behavior with someone in the church but have resisted.

- 34% of pastors wrestle with the temptation of pornography or visit pornographic sites.

- 57% of pastors feel fulfilled but yet discouraged, stressed, and fatigued.

- 84% of pastors desire to have close fellowship with someone they can trust and confide in.

- Over 50% of pastors are unhealthy, overweight, and do not exercise.

- The profession of "Pastor" is near the bottom of a survey of the most-respected professions, just above "car salesman."

- Many denominations are reporting an "Empty Pulpit Crisis." They do not have a shortage of ministers but have a shortage of ministers desiring to fill the role of a pastor.

- 71% of churches have no plan for a pastor to receive a periodic sabbatical.

- 30% of churches have no documentation clearly outlining what the church expects of their pastor.

- 1 out of every 10 pastors will actually retire as a pastor.

Let me make up a statistic: 65% of pastors who just read that list are looking for a bottle of strychnine to drink. I jest, but that list is truly discouraging.

Is ministry meant to be drudgery? Are preachers of the gospel intended to flounder for decades, being used and abused, run down, washed up, burned out and finally thrown on a heap of ministerial rubbish? Or, is there a way to flourish in ministry, victoriously enjoying and embracing the unending challenges, long hours and impossible situations with vitality and reward?

I say without any reservation to the last question, YES! Consider a sampling of the promises of our good God to His servants:

- *"Go ye therefore and make disciples... and lo, I am with you always." (Matthew 28:19, 20)* Jesus gave a job and He gave a promise.

- *"I will never leave you nor forsake you." (Hebrews 13:5)*

- *"I will go before you." (Mark 14:28)*

- *"Be strong and of a good courage; be not afraid, neither be thou dismayed: for the LORD thy God is with thee whithersoever thou goest." (Joshua 1:9)*

- *"I am the vine, ye are the branches: He that abideth in me, and I in him, the same bringeth forth much fruit: for without me ye can do nothing. Without me ye can do nothing." (John 15:5)*

- *"But ye shall receive power after that the Holy Ghost is come upon you." (Acts 1:8)*. Here it is in Acts, our docking station, where the power is provided; none other than the Holy Ghost of God.

With that in mind, let's look with fresh eyes at the fruit of the Spirit:

"But the fruit of the Spirit is love, joy, peace, longsuffering, gentleness, goodness, faith, Meekness, temperance: against such there is no law. And they that are Christ's have crucified the flesh with the affections and lusts. If we live in the Spirit, let us also walk in the Spirit." (Galatians 5:22-25)

Isn't this the expectation we had when we surrendered to ministry? Did we not believe that ministry would be loving, joyful and peaceful? Weren't we expecting a life of patience, gentleness and goodness?

Those resources are readily available to the weary warrior of the cross by regular reconnection to our power supply.

A simple, sincere prayer never fails to re-energize me: "Father, cleanse me of me and fill me with your Holy Spirit. I want to be used of You in whatever manner you see best. I can't do this on my own, I need you to do it through me. Thanks for the filling of your sweet Spirit. Amen."

Showers of Blessing

The shower tends to be a prayer closet for me.

I've been an adult for nearly sixteen thousand days. I try to shower daily, so how much more routine can something get after 16,000 times? It's pretty mindless stuff. Soap, rinse, shampoo, rinse, dry off. Ho-hum.

I can pretty much pray in the shower without interference. Electronic distractions are clearly out of the question. You may find that shocking. Only problem, I've always been mindful of conserving time and water, so, a shower is generally a brief proposition for me. Nevertheless, some one-on-one with God normally transpires in the streamed, steamed cubicle.

In that cleansing holy of holies, I was recently contemplating, with the Holy Spirit's help, why and how so much grief can come upon a person at once. I was deeply concerned about my wife's health as well as the abuse she'd been suffering on the job the past several months at the hands of an unscrupulous person. Then there was the church member who texted me that he's a better father than god (small "g") ever was and that he was through with God. The same day there was the horrible, shocking news of sexual abuse of a little girl of our church. To add to the misery, there had been a sexual assault of one of our new converts by, of all people, another one of our new "converts." There was more, but let's let those tragedies suffice as an example. 48 hours of agonizing for a pastor whose sheep and family mean so much to him. These were not little foxes that were spoiling my vines. They were full sized wolves devouring my world. I found myself disheartened and depleted.

In the steady streams of the refreshing waters, the Lord reminded me that the enemy is pulling out all the stops. His modus operandi is constant; steal, kill and destroy. He reminded me that the several souls that came to faith because of the gospel in the previous few days caused Slew Foot to step up his game. The greasy goblin's kingdom was under attack and he wanted to remind me how much more comfortable it was to just go with the flow and don't ruffle spiritual feathers. The enemy often parlays with me, offering a truce: "Go with the flow and I'll leave you alone."

A minister worth his salt can make no such bargain! He must actively storm the gates of hell, robbing the pit of its future inhabitants, plucking the brands from the burning.

But so much concentrated grief and pain! So, I asked the Lord, as I applied the shampoo, what should I do? How can I help these people in their afflictions? He nudged me to ensure that my robo-vac was securely affixed to its base so that it was receiving it's full charge. I'm not talking allegory here. I literally rinsed, dried off, checked my little robot friend and, sure enough, it wasn't being charged. Even though it was on its base, there wasn't a proper connection.

"Loud and clear, Lord. I get it!"

I realized that even though I could check all the boxes: reading the Word, praying, serving, giving, working, attending, etc., that I had been docking out of "have to" rather than "want to." The connection with my heavenly Power Source was weak. Sure enough, between me justifying myself regarding sin I was just going through the motions. I wasn't really connecting well.

Have you ever mindlessly eaten a fantastic steak dinner and later realized and regretted not even savoring the awesomeness of the meal? You sat at the table, chewed and swallowed the meat, but you never became the complete connoisseur. Afterwards, you felt as if you wasted a meal because you were merely eating to eat, rather than dining to enjoy.

Such can be our connection, or lack thereof, with our Power Source. We do what we have to do, because that's what we do. But shouldn't we be completely plugged in, enjoying the recharge in which the Lord is infusing into us as we fellowship with Him, drinking of the water of life, ingesting the bread of life, meanwhile tasting and seeing that the Lord is exceedingly good? Of course, we should. This is another reason why so many ministers are functionally discharged. They are not returning to base and fully connecting.

And with so many carpets yet to clean!!!

Here's your reminder, the work of the ministry is too hard, its duration too long, its disappointments too deep, its pitfalls too many for us to do it without regularly recharging. Return to your dock often.

66 Practical things to Help you Recharge

1. Get away regularly, unplugging as you do.

2. Take up a hobby.

3. Sign up for a side gig.

4. Romance your spouse.

5. Relax.

6. Reflect.

7. Smile and laugh more, worry less.

8. Exercise.

9. Do some volunteer stuff.

10. Take a walk.

11. Cast your cares upon Him.

12. Rest in the Beloved.

13. Read.

14. Pray.

15. Catch a movie and buy the big popcorn.

16. Memorize Psalm 16:11

17. Cheer your team (all-out yelling for them).

18. Watch a classic comedy movie.

19. Watch a tear-jerking film.

20. Get enough sleep.

21. Engage a stranger in conversation.

22. Fast from social media.

23. Visit the hospital.

24. Put the phone down.

25. Give God praise.

26. Shout "Amen!" and "Hallelujah!" in church.

27. Shout "Amen!" outside of church.

28. Give your spouse a real kiss more often.

29. Tell people you love them.

30. Do a police/fire ride-along.

31. Take a mission's trip.

32. Love someone who isn't very lovely.

33. Sing like you mean it, and God deserves it.

34. Hand a homeless person a $5 bill.

35. Write a thank you note.

36. Visit a nursing home.

37. Make peace between estranged people.

38. Forgive somebody.

39. Let a hurt be forgotten.

40. Do some therapeutic shopping.

41. Play a round of golf.

42. Shoot a gun.

43. Ride a motorcycle.

44. Lay out under the clouds and imagine shapes.

45. Do a crossword puzzle.

46. Put a puzzle together.

47. Look through old family photos.

48. Hand-wash the car.

49. Garden.

50. Do your spouse's chores.

51. Attend a concert.

52. Call someone you've not seen in forever.

53. Ask someone how you can pray for them.

54. Sit out under the stars and give the Creator glory.

55. Go garage-saling.

56. Take a cruise.

57. Bless a missionary.

58. Compliment someone in sincerity.

59. Mentor a needy child.

60. Take a new believer under your wing.

61. Meditate.

62. Eat ice cream. No one ever did so with a frown.

63. Visit the cemetery.

64. Take a nap.

65. Win a soul.

66. Get filled with the Holy Spirit.

Dr. Gary Fuller is a police and fire chaplain and the founding pastor of Gentle Shepherd in Lincoln, Nebraska, the church he planted in his hometown over two decades ago. He has been a college professor, music evangelist, camp director, and most important, husband and father to a wonderful family.

TAKE PAUL'S ADVICE

Jerry Pelfrey

THE BLESSINGS INHERITED through Christ are beyond measure and comprehension. One of these blessings is our access to the ancient texts written by the Apostle Paul. His letters are true treasures… and treasures, by their very nature, are meant to be pursued, discovered, and shared.

As an apostle, Paul had an extraordinary position. He had a unique personal experience with the risen Savior, he was given commissioned authority directly from Christ, and he had the inspiration of the Holy Spirit in his writings. We know that, other than Christ, no one had greater concern for the Church than Paul. His visible and constant care and compassion for God's people are beyond compare.

An example of his vigilant care for the Church is found in his letter to the believers in Colossae.

> *"For I want you to know what a great conflict I have for you
> and those in Laodicea, and for as many as have not seen
> my face in the flesh, 2 that their hearts may be encouraged,
> being knit together in love, and attaining to all riches of
> the full assurance of understanding, to the knowledge of the
> mystery of God, both of the Father and of Christ, 3 in whom*

are hidden all the treasures of wisdom and knowledge."
(Colossians 2:1-4)

The word "conflict" used in this passage comes from the Greek word "agon," which is our English word for agony. Paul wanted the church in Colossae, and in the neighboring communities, to know that he agonized over them for the cause of Christ. This ever-consuming nature of ministry gives us insight as to why Paul would write the following to Timothy.

> *"Take heed to yourself and to the doctrine. Continue in them,*
> *for in doing this you will save both yourself and those who*
> *hear you." (1 Timothy 4:16)*

"Take heed" means to watch closely and carefully over your personal, spiritual, physical, and emotional health. Paul communicated to young Timothy that he should never be too busy to care for his body, soul and spirit and always be diligent to guard the truth. Timothy's work held eternal consequences, and he would one day give an account of this work on judgment day.

So, what advice and warnings would Paul give if he were able to critique our westernized 21st century Christianity?

Let's imagine if Paul, just for a day, could attend and give counsel to a group of modern-day American pastors gathered together at a conference. If he were given an open mic what would he say? Undoubtedly there would be justifiable rebuke, and we could only hope that it would be brief. From there he would speak from his heart and then open the floor for Q and A about life and ministry. An excellent first question is then asked from the audience,"What is the most crucial advice you could give us as pastors?" Paul might answer, "There are three things you should never underestimate... our spiritual enemy, the depravity of our heart and the death-defying power of our risen Savior."

His explanation would then follow something like this....

Never Underestimate the Deception of our Spiritual Enemy

"Finally, my brethren, be strong in the Lord and in the power of His might. Put on the whole armor of God, that you may be able to stand against the wiles of the devil. For we do not wrestle against flesh and blood, but against principalities, against powers, against the rulers of the darkness of this age, against spiritual hosts of wickedness in the heavenly places. Therefore take up the whole armor of God, that you may be able to withstand in the evil day, and having done all, to stand." (Ephesians 6:10-13)

Do not be fooled. Satan is far from being haphazard. He is methodical and purposeful. He despises any thought of God being glorified. Satan is a lion with a mission to devour the faith of Christ followers. Although he is a lion held on a leash by our sovereign God, our enemy has liberty on this side of his final judgment. Pastors, take heed on every front... with your friendships and fellow pastors, (2 Corinthians 11:13-15), the counsel you provide, (1 Timothy 5:14-15, 2 Timothy 2:24-26), your personal and family life (2 Corinthians 2:8-11, Ephesians 4:27, 1 Timothy 3:5-6), your ministry in and out of the pulpit, (2 Thessalonians 2:18), and your bedroom. (1

Corinthians 7:5) Your enemy is eager to deceive, damage, and even destroy your trust and hope in Christ using every possible means to devour you. Protect and enjoy your sex life, guard against holding grudges, do not carry your frustration and hurt over to the next day, be compassionate with sin-loving people, show concern to the vulnerable widows, be disciplined in your thought life, and express patience and humility to fellow pastors. Guard your words carefully, for you are a master of the words you keep, but a servant to the words you speak. Be a diligent student of this enemy; your spiritual wellbeing depends upon alertness.

Never Underestimate the Depravity of our Heart

We are redeemed in Jesus Christ, therefore, we can rejoice. However, it is easy to underestimate the negative effect of the fall of Adam. Depravity runs deep. Because of the fall of man-kind, our thoughts and emotions are not trustworthy. God does not tell us to ignore reason and feelings but warns us to proceed with caution. Our hearts will deceive us and betray Christ without hesitation. It is written, *"He who trusts in his own heart is a fool, But whoever walks wisely will be delivered." (Proverbs 28:26)*

Our love for Christ is not without competition, for temptations are an overflow of our fallen nature. During the sanctification process, it will not take long to discover that it is much easier to be selfish than selfless. The sweet psalmist of Israel knew his heart was set on God, yet it had the capacity to turn away from God. He wrote, *"With my whole heart I have sought You; Oh, let me not wander from Your commandments!" (Psalm 119:10)*.

Paul revealed his experience as an apostle who struggled with the depravity of his heart to the believers in Rome. He confessed that the things he desired to practice he failed to pull off, and the things he desired to avoid, he yielded to (Romans 7). Our flesh can never be taught and will fake submission. It has the potential and ability to commit treason against Christ at any moment. The tension between loving Christ and loving self is real, and it is powerful.

"I say then: Walk in the Spirit, and you shall not fulfill the lust of the flesh. 17 For the flesh lusts against the Spirit, and the Spirit against the flesh; and these are contrary to one another, so that you do not do the things that you wish." (Galatians 5:16-17)

Remember Abraham's pressure to protect his own life at the loss of Sarah's security and integrity. Why would such a man of faith yield in this manner, not once, but on two occasions? The answer is the depravity of the heart. Or what of David, who being a man after God's own heart, fell into adultery and murder. Or what of David's son, Solomon, who had greater insight into life than anyone, yet turned away to years of folly. What of Jonah who could not rejoice in the salvation of the heathen? Behavior and attitudes may vary, but the answer is the same. Lovers of God yield to such sin because of the depravity of the heart. Do not trust your heart in the best of circumstances or fall into despair at the worst of them. Take heed unto yourself!

Never Underestimate the Death-defying Power of our Risen Savior

If we stopped at points one and two, we would live how those without Christ live, in hopelessness. We would be at the mercy of our spiritual enemy and the depravity of our heart, neither of which shows us any form of grace. Therefore, never underestimate the death-defying power of Christ. Without His resurrection, our faith is worthless. As preachers of the gospel, we would be found liars, we would have no rescue from our sins, and we would be the most miserable people on the planet (1Corinthians 15). However, the death-defying power of our risen Lord means we have a hope that has no equal. Christ is our Savior, our Advocate, our High Priest, and our coming King. When our enemy gains spiritual territory within our lives and our heart condemns us, our advocate, Christ Jesus, does His perfect work on our behalf. He empowers us against our spiritual enemy and enables us to submit to obedience and walk in holiness. Every good work that we accomplish for the glory of God is a result of the grace found in our risen Savior. Our works do not pay God back; they borrow more on our risen Savior's grace, which places us in greater debt. Our theme throughout eternity will be the grace of God through our risen Savior, and eternity will not be long enough for us to praise God for all that He has done.

"Therefore I also, after I heard of your faith in the Lord Jesus and your love for all the saints, do not cease to give thanks for you, making mention of you in my prayers: that the God of our Lord Jesus Christ, the Father of glory, may give to you the spirit of wisdom and revelation in the knowledge of Him, the eyes of your understanding being enlightened; that

*you may know what is the hope of His calling, what are
the riches of the glory of His inheritance in the saints, and
what is the exceeding greatness of His power toward us
who believe, according to the working of His mighty power
which He worked in Christ when He raised Him from the
dead and seated Him at His right hand in the heavenly
places, far above all principality and power and might
and dominion, and every name that is named, not only
in this age but also in that which is to come. And He put
all things under His feet, and gave Him to be head over
all things to the church, which is His body, the fullness of
Him who fills all in all." (Ephesians 1:15-23)*

Take heed unto yourself, for all who live godly in Christ will
suffer persecution. Many outside America are experiencing
grievous aggressive and physical persecution. However, you
should not minimize the suffering that westernized pastors
face, though it is milder. Westernized suffering is experienced through slander and rejection. It is emotional. Not recognizing this suffering limits your ability to rejoice in the
midst of trials, and opens the door for potential discouragement and self-pity. Take heed, you will have trials without
and temptations within. At times, they are ever present and
can be overwhelming. You will experience personal rejection,
deep disappointment, and severe desperation that will appear
unbearable. Quite frankly, your heart will be broken. You will
discover that your commitment to ministry will not sustain
you. You will need something greater, richer. You will need to
rest in the death-defying power of our risen Lord as defined in
Ephesians 1:20 - *"... according to the working of His mighty
power which He worked in Christ when He raised Him from*

the dead!" In Christ, you will discover your suffering can be endured and will one day be celebrated.

So whether the Apostle Paul stood before fishermen, shepherds, religionists, moralists, pagans, philosophers, political leaders, scholars, laity or fellow elders, his message was single-focused and always the same, the risen Christ. He had no small print or hidden agendas in his letters or in his sermons. His theme in word and life was and still is the risen Lord. He did not fear death; he welcomed it. He knew that absence from his body meant presence with his Lord. But he did fear that his sermons would lead some to trust in men rather than put their faith in God.

> *"And I, brethren, when I came to you, did not come with excellence of speech or of wisdom declaring to you the testimony of God. For I determined not to know anything among you except Jesus Christ and Him crucified. I was with you in weakness, in fear, and in much trembling. And my speech and my preaching were not with persuasive words of human wisdom, but in demonstration of the Spirit and of power, that your faith should not be in the wisdom of men but in the power of God." (1 Corinthians 2:1-5)*

Paul's words today to pastors might very well be:

As our Lord's servant and apostle, I urge you as God's leaders to never underestimate the deception of our spiritual enemy, the depravity of our heart, and the death-defying power of our risen Savior. *"Take heed to yourself and to the doctrine. Continue in them, for in doing this you will save both yourself and those who hear you." (1 Timothy 4:16). "Therefore, my beloved brethren, be steadfast, immovable, always abounding in the work of the Lord, knowing that your labor is not in vain in the Lord" (1 Corinthians 15:58)*

Jerry Pelfrey and Char married in 1979. They have four daughters and eleven grandchildren. Both are graduates from Baptist Bible College in Springfield, Mo. Jerry graduated from Liberty University, MAR. Served in youth ministry for five years and has been lead Pastor of Grace Baptist Church in Mason, Ohio since 1985. He served as Director of RUSH Student Ministry Camp for 14 years. Jerry and Char are active within their community. Char served on Mason City Council for 16 years and one term as Mayor. Both are members of the Kiwanis Civic organization where Jerry served as President and is a long time member of Mason Police and Fire Chaplaincy program.

Develop Some Pastor Priorities

Linzy Slayden

SOME PEOPLE INSTINCTIVELY know what their priorities are. The classified section of the Quay County Sun newspaper in June of 1978 contained this ad: "Farmer with 160 irrigated acres wants marriage minded woman with tractor. When replying, please send picture of the tractor." That is someone who knows his priorities!

One of the first things I learned in the pastorate was to set priorities. If you don't learn this discipline, ministry can become more confusing and complicated then it needs to be.

When the Apostle Paul was writing his last letter from a Roman prison, as the parchment was filling up, he had some very important things to say to the young preacher, Timothy. He was helping Timothy with some priorities,

"I charge thee therefore before God, and the Lord Jesus Christ, who shall judge the quick and the dead at his appearing and his kingdom; Preach the word; be instant in season, out of season; reprove, rebuke, exhort with all long suffering and doctrine. For the time will come when they will not endure

sound doctrine; but after their own lusts shall they heap to themselves teachers, having itching ears; And they shall turn away their ears from the truth, and shall be turned unto fables." (II Timothy 4:1-4)

Not long ago I was asked to talk about what I have learned about pastoring and preaching from nearly 40 years of ministry. I thought long about the answer and the Lord gave me six priorities that I needed for my ministry. These are broad brush strokes to consider.

Foundation... Essential for a Strong Ministry

The first thing for a long and effective ministry is to develop a foundation.

When we talk about foundation it must include a few areas. There must be a foundation of character. This qualifies us or disqualifies us from ministry. It will determine at what level we minister (Psalm 11:3). The biblical criteria for pastors are mostly character issues. I have seen that what can be built by a powerful charismatic personality can be destroyed by lack of personal character. I think character is your life message. The Lord is intent on making you a message as well as giving you a message. Character is something formed in us by godly influence, godly upbringing (although this aspect can be overcome), discipline, trials, stresses, mentoring, and sensitivity to God and His Word. The little things in life are important. It's the "little foxes that spoil the vines" (Song of Solomon 2:15).

That being said, I also think we need a foundation of education and training. This gives us content in ministry life. This is a reference to wisdom, knowledge, and insight gained through experience, study and training. This keeps us from running like Ahimaaz who wanted to run with zeal but no clear message. (II Samuel 18:19ff).

Most of the great Bible characters spent years of preparation to develop "content" in their "ministry" life. When I left my job at John Deere in Moline, Illinois, I wanted a foundation for a life-long ministry. When I got to Baptist Bible College in Springfield, MO, I signed up for the hardest professors I could because I didn't leave my life in Illinois to play games in ministry. I wanted to be challenged. I wanted to learn. I wanted to be effective. I was told I was crazy but it helped me to have a great foundation of disciplined study that I knew I would need the rest of my ministry life. I was not raised in a Christian home. I remember going to church only a handful of times growing up, so I knew I needed the education and training.

Along with a great education, I needed some "on the job" training. I found that mentoring, practical experience, and personal discipleship as an associate pastor helped prepare me for a long ministry. I personally believe every pastor should be an associate first. It gives a great perspective for team building in the ministry. Whereas character qualifies a good minister, content adds wisdom for ministry.

Your foundation develops your capacity. Capacity not only involves knowing what you know, it helps you realize where to go for what you don't know. It helps you understand how you are gifted and knowing your strengths and weaknesses so we can move toward fulfilling our full measure and potential in serving the Lord.

Faith... Faith Pleases God

The second thing I found I needed was to do as one man said, "Dig my faith well deep." I am reminded what the writer of Hebrews says, *"But without faith it is impossible to please God: for he that cometh to God must believe that he is, and that he is a rewarder of them that diligently seek him" (Hebrews 11:6).*

Ministry is the greatest calling in life! Wonderful things happen. But along with those great exciting moments come challenges. Guaranteed! Therefore we need to dig that faith well deep! During the ministry journey, we find it necessary to dip into that faith well often. Life and ministry will challenge our faith. Things can change in a flash. We don't want the faith well to dry up when it's needed the most.

My ministry calling took me from my home in the Land of Lincoln to the Ozark hills of Missouri and then further southwest to Tulsa, Oklahoma. Along the way I needed a growing faith. I thought I understood about faith when I resigned my job at John Deere after eight years, took my little family and headed to Baptist Bible College. I found out my faith would be challenged in a greater way than I expected. I was called foolish for leaving my job at John Deere for not knowing where I would end up. The Lord provided every step of the way, but not without much concern on my part and hard lessons in prayer and faith. I had never been on my knees begging God like I learned to do the first year of Bible college. The Lord provided just enough part-time work to get by and the second semester I found the job that I would keep my entire time. As the school years went by, I found that the Lord could move on the hearts of folks to help us as the needs surfaced. This was a humbling and hard part of my faith walk but it helped me to understand the faithfulness of the Lord when I got in full-time ministry. I found that the lessons learned then have helped as an associate pastor and later as lead pastor. One professor, Dr. Gillming, used to say, 'You can't traffic in unlearned truths."

The fact is, ministry is too unpredictable to be motivated by security, It's too unprofitable to be motivated by money. It's too demanding to be motivated by pleasure. It's too criticized to be motivated by fame. Our ministry should be motived by the pleasure of God, and God is pleased when we have ministry powered by faith.

Focus... Watch the Comparison Traps... Be Yourself

Comparing with others is part of human nature. This is seen in Luke 18 when the Pharisee and the tax collector went up to the Temple to pray and one was self righteous and the other repentant. The self righteous Pharisee compared himself with the repentant tax collector.

Comparison is an easy and subtle trap to fall into in any field of work; but especially for men of God. As ministers of the gospel, each may have different spiritual gifts, or some may have privileges others may not have. We compare, contrast, and weigh our ministries by the successes, failures, and expectations of others. Regardless of your stage or level of ministry, this temptation is a persistent foe. The overachiever in us wants to excel and advance. We want to win souls, build buildings, grow ministries, speak frequently, minister often, and increase our network. However, some men, in the name of ministry, are simply trying to make a name for themselves. If we are not careful, we will compare and contrast our lives with others and, thus, affect our motivation for what we do.

Our success or failure is not determined by another's experience; it is measured by our obedience to God's Word and acceptance to God's will.

When we compare our ministries with others, one of two things will happen. We will either be full of pride or full of pity. We will be full of pride if we are doing "better" than the next guy. Yet, we will be full of self pity if we fall short of his success. The Lord doesn't want our ministries to be characterized by either one of these mindsets.

God doesn't give everyone the same ministry. Noah had a building ministry. Moses had a shepherding ministry. David had a writing and singing ministry. Paul had a church planting ministry. We all have particular tasks and assignments that are ordained by God. Most of the time we get in trouble when we covet what God has allocated to others.

My true measure of success is my obedience and faithfulness to Christ. If it is His will for me to pastor 30, 300 or 3,000 people, I must commit my allegiance and affection to that plan, regardless of its size. In doing that, I have fulfilled my ultimate duty – submission to God's will and design for my life.

The comparison trap is one thing, but learning and observing others is different. We can and should learn from others without falling into the comparison trap. Let's keep our eyes on Jesus.

Family... No Gospel Orphans

As pastors, we are men in our community. And as such, the Scripture identifies us more often than not as being married men, and married men more often than not have children. When the congregation is instructed from the Word to look for men for the work of pastoring, they are told that one of the things they are to look for in a man is his relation to his family. A congregation will recognize who is capable of leadership in the church by recognizing those leadership skills being exercised in the man's home.

The way a man loves and leads in his home will be in large measure the same way that he will love and lead in the church. The skills that he has to lead his wife and children are the same skills that will then be applied in giving leadership to the people of God. Unlike any other vocation or job that men may have, the family is vital for the effectiveness of a minister.

One would never go to work in a secular environment and have a boss ask, "So how's your marriage?" He doesn't care much. If you're selling widgets and gadgets, he just wants you to sell as many widgets and gadgets as you can. If your marriage is a mess, it doesn't matter, as long as you're selling widgets and gadgets. Your boss would never ask "How are your children?" Again, it doesn't matter to him, just as long as you're being productive on the workplace.

The minister's job is not like that. If a minister fails at home, he is out of a job, if you will. What a minister is as a man is most evident in his own home. If a man is not a Christian in his home, he's not a Christian. If a man is not a Christian in his marriage, he's not a Christian. If he's not a Christian in his family, he's not a Christian. A pastor's primary relationships are indicators for the church to observe. Paul tells us, *"If a man know not how to rule his own house, how shall he take care of the church of God?' (I Timothy 3:5)* The bottom line is that your family is important and needs to be a priority. It takes effort and time and creativity, but it can be and needs to be done.

Friends... Help Along the Way... Networking

Friendships in ministry matters! I am reminded that one of the most powerful tools in any industry is networking, and it's no different in ministry. The reality is that we were not created to do ministry alone. Networking helps on several levels.

It helps us with inspiration. We are constantly faced with the calling of staying ahead of our people, staying fresh in our relationship with the Lord, and always improving and being creative in our ministry. We need others to speak wisdom, insight, and ideas in every season of ministry life.

It also helps with accountability. We all need accountability. It helps prevent the development of bad habits that are dangerous to our ministry and family. Meeting others and discussing ministry ideas and challenges is not only enjoyable, it helps keep our focus where it ought to be.

A developed network helps in emergency times in ministry life. Four years ago, our four-year old grandson was diagnosed with cancer and I was blessed by the broad network of pastors, teachers, missionaries across our fellowship that had special prayer for him. Knowing we had a worldwide prayer team not only helped him but our entire family. It made a difference!

Finishing Strong

We've all known people in ministry who seemed to have it all together when suddenly everything imploded. Maybe it surfaced in an affair, or, in many cases, just from pure exhaustion, burnout and frustration. (People can be frustrating!) On the other hand, we've seen people explode across the finish line with energy to burn. What's the difference?

I find myself in the 6th decade of life and approaching the 4th decade in ministry. It's easy to see that there is more road behind me than there is in front of me. While no one knows the number of his days, there is the likelihood I could have several years yet to serve the Lord. As the steward of my life and the ministry God has given me, how will I invest these remaining years? I want to finish strong in life and ministry.

According to Bob Buford in *Finishing Well*, as most people approach mid-life they are unprepared and are still seeking for purpose. That should not be the case for the man of God. Our purpose pushes us and carries us until we see the Lord face to face. To do that, we need to be reminded that relationships are key. When you boil life down to its barest essence, it's about relationships. Our relationship to God, spouse, family, and friends.

John Maxwell once said that on our deathbed we will not wish we had spent more time at the office. I agree. I have been at the bedside of people in their last moments and I have never heard anyone say they should have worked more. Relationships are extremely important and they should be kept in good repair.

Along with that emphasis, we should be lifelong learners. When we cease to be curious and to learn, we cease to grow and then we begin to die. The late Howard Hendricks stated that the average person dies between two and seven years after retirement because they have lost their purpose in life. For most, their purpose was wrapped up in their work. Once work is done, they have no meaning in their lives.

For the child of God, especially the pastor, our mission in life can change but we still live on mission. I want to continue to help others achieve their purpose and be involved in a cause that lives beyond me. We may need to prepare ourselves for changing seasons of life. Howard Hendricks once prayed, "Lord, help me not die before I die."

God help us to stay faithful to the Word of God, faithful to our wives and families, keep personal purity and walk humbly before our God.

These are valuable lessons that I learned in my ministry and, if time travel were available, I would tell my younger self and others many things about pastoral ministry but no one has invented the Flux Capacitor (if you have to ask, watch *Back to the Future*) or the Quantum Realm with Pym Particles (See *Avengers: Endgame*) so I can't talk to folks in the past. But I can talk to others today, and perhaps I can help those involved in the greatest work in the world (the ministry) to be more joyful and effective.

Linzy Slayden has pastored Friendship Baptist Church of Owasso, Oklahoma for 27 years. He has degrees from Baptist Bible College, Springfield, MO. and Temple Baptist Seminary, Chattanooga, TN. He is a two-time President of the Baptist Bible Fellowship International. He and Carla have been married 46 years with four married children and they enjoy 12 grandchildren. They reside in Owasso, Oklahoma.

Keep Family a Priority

Sam Keller

WE FACED MANY cultural and personal adjustments when we arrived in Perth, Western Australia in 1973. I had just spent a year and a half on the road in America raising the support we needed to start new churches in Australia. We had literally transferred our family into a strange new world.

It all reminds me of a TV program called Sliders that aired several years ago. The series follows a group of travelers as they use a wormhole to "slide" between different parallel universes. This wormhole would appear and disappear at random times and it was like being picked up by a huge vacuum cleaner from one universe, sliding through a big tube and spit out in a very different world.

That is very much the way we felt when we tried to get settled in our new home. Things that we had done all our lives suddenly became a bit more complicated. Buying groceries, going to one shop for dairy products, to another one for vegetables, and to another for bread which had to be bought every day because it was without preservatives. Driving on the other side of the street, which got exciting when we bought our VW van and set out the first time on our own. We were not sure where we were and how to get to where we needed to be.

This transition not only related to the cultural world, but also to our family. I had not spent much time with my family during the time I was raising support. They had stayed at our home and I had traveled alone most of the time. When I resigned as pastor of the church we had started, our income dropped to zero, so I had to start immediately. The first time I left, I was gone 8 weeks and my wife and two daughters stayed home so they could attend school. It was like that for a year and a half.

For many years I was puzzled and confused as to what were the most important things in my life. As a pastor and missionary, I knew that my ministry was very important. I worked hard at that. I did not take time for my family and other things that were also important because I was concerned that God would not be pleased if I did not succeed in my ministry. I had been taught that if I took care of the ministry, God would take care of my family.

Yet as I looked around at some of the most successful pastors and missionaries, they were losing their family, their kids were bitter toward the ministry, wives were unhappy because the husband never seemed to have time for her or their children. I am not overly brilliant, but somehow that did not make sense. If they were so successful, why were they losing their family?

So, in a strange new world, and in a unfamiliar lifestyle, how are we going to handle life in general and particularly family life? What is our first responsibility? How will we tend to the needs of family and do the work the Lord had called us to half-way around the world?

God is our first priority. Nothing should come before God. But there are many things we could state as our second priority. What do you think He would want as our second priority, second to only Him? What comes next after God? How about our kids, our ministry, prayer, spouse, our job, private time, other people, our church attendance or participation, our own health and well-being? We can get some idea of where our family fits in by realizing that, after a personal relationship with us, God instituted the relationship of the family.

Our second priority is the relationship we have with our family, our spouse and our children. And in the New Testament He tells us:

> *"But if any provide not for his own, and specially for those of his own house, he hath denied the faith, and is worse than an infidel." (1 Timothy 5:8)*

There are many who get confused between the family and their work, whether it is in the ministry or in the business world. They think and say, "I work and do my job because I love my family and it proves my love for them. I try to provide for them and give them the best I can." But, how many times have we seen work-alcoholics in the ministry or business world lose their family because they did not take time for them. They did not provide the most important thing that was needed by their family — themselves. Things will never replace people and a loving relationship. If you did not have a family, you would still work at a job; they are not the only reason you work.

There are many who mistake their ministry with their relationship with God. Our relationship with God has never and will never be based on what we do for Him. It can only be based on what God has done for us. He sent His Son that we might have life and forgiveness of sin, become the children of God, or however you want to describe it. Our obedience to Him will never conflict with the responsibility we have to our family unless something is wrong with one or the other.

Some would think that our obedience defines our relationship to God. Our obedience is a product of that relationship, not the source of it. The important thing to remember is that God will never put our obedience to Him in conflict with our responsibility to our family. If there is a conflict, it is there because we have not understood what the two relationships are, and how we are to fulfill both.

Let me illustrate what I am saying. Just before we left for Australia we were told that our daughter had abilities in gymnastics that should be developed. When we were settled into a house and ready to start the work that God had called us to do there, we investigated the opportunities for her in this area. We found a coach who was a member of the Australian Olympic Gymnastic team and was taking students. It would involve a one-way trip of about 45 minutes, about 2-3 hours of training and another 45-minute drive back home. This was 3 days a week and then sometimes on Saturday.

Yes, it was a lot of time to commit to something that was, after all, just a sport or hobby. But, I promised my daughter that I would do all that I could to see that we could take advantage of this opportunity. So, on those three days a week, I would pick her up from the train station, since she rode it an hour one way to school and then back in the afternoon. We would then set out for the gym and she would train with the team. I would wait there, because if I had gone back home, I would have had to return almost as soon as I got there. I took along the things I would need to study and would sit in the back of our VW van and study for 2-3 hours. We usually got home just in time for a late dinner.

This all worked very well until we started our church and it grew and the responsibilities of pastoring grew. Our Sunday School grew to the point that we had classes for almost every age and had teachers for these classes. We also had a man who was the Sunday School superintendent. He decided that we needed to have a monthly teachers meeting to work with and help train the teachers. I agreed that it was a great idea. One problem was that he wanted me to be at this meeting and take part in the plans and training. I said, "Sorry, I can't be there" because this was going to be on a night that I took my daughter to gymnastics and I would not be back until the class was nearly over. He did not understand and questioned my priorities. He said the Lord's work was a lot more important than any sport or hobby. And, he was right, but there was no activity that was more important than my daughter, and I had promised to support her. So my daughter took precedence over the teachers meeting.

The man who is now pastor of that church has told me several times that, when this all happened, he could not understand why I did what I did. But now he understands and he has tried to do the same with his family.

It could be that your family is making unreasonable demands on you. This can happen when we do not have the right priorities. But if we establish where everything fits into our lives, and help them understand what the right order should be, it will help with those unreasonable demands. This is why it is so important to marry the right spouse. They need to understand your commitment to God and have the same level of commitment to Him. If you practice putting God as your first priority and your spouse does also, there will never be a conflict that cannot be worked out. I am sure that God will honor such commitment and help in your relationship with your spouse.

The Priority for a Minister's Spouse

The instructions husbands are given are very clear. *"Husbands, love your wives, even as Christ also loved the church, and gave himself for it; That he might sanctify and cleanse it with the washing of water by the word, That he might present it to himself a glorious church, not having spot, or wrinkle, or any such thing; but that it should be holy and without blemish."* (Ephesians 5:25-27)

John MacArthur says in his commentary on Ephesians: "For husbands to love their wives as Christ loves His church is to love them with a purifying love (emphasis added). Divine love does not simply condemn wrong in those loved, but seeks to cleanse them from it." He goes on to say: "Love wants only the best for the one it loves, and it cannot bear for a loved one to be corrupted or misled by anything evil or harmful. When a husband's love for his wife is like Christ's love for His church, he will continually seek to help purify her from any sort of defilement. He will seek to protect her from the world's contamination and protect her holiness, virtue, and purity in every way. He will never induce her to do that which is wrong or unwise or expose her to that which is less than good."

The wife's relationship with God is really hers and she should guard it with great care. But the husband should not allow anything in their family life that would lead her astray. He is to be the example, the guardian and the protector of things in the home. By his example, the entire family should see what a relationship with God should look like.

It is not required of you to be responsible for their relationship with God. If you are setting the right example, and being obedient to Him, He will honor that and help you work out the problems. It has well been said by Theodore Hesburgh, "the greatest gift a father can give his children is to love their mother."

To have this kind of love is to set the right example in your own standing with the Lord. It is to have tough love if it is necessary. It is to help with constructive suggestions, rather than with a critical or demanding attitude. It is allowing criticism to be directed toward you. Ministers are not perfect. Even if you never admit it, the wife and children know they are not even anywhere near perfection. But, when a minister admits to being wrong, it shows that being wrong happens to everyone and will give greater confidence to the rest of the family.

It is not a matter that your spouse, or your children do what they are supposed to do before you do what you are supposed to do. It is rather a matter of you fulfilling your obligations to God and your family as an example. I know this is true, because it worked in my marriage. It was not me that did the right thing, but my wonderful wife. She surrendered her life to God, to be the right kind of wife for me no matter what I did.

I had been taught by others that if I just took care of "my ministry" and worked hard for God, He would take care of my family, and they should understand that the most important thing was working and pleasing Him. They should understand that "my ministry" was what I did for Him, and He came before everything else.

"My ministry" was the most important thing in my life because I did not understand that my standing with God was based on what He had done for me, not what I was doing for Him. When these two were sorted out, "my ministry" became something very wonderful. It was neither a burden nor something difficult that I had to do. It was a joyful product of my standing with God. Also, I found that my work for the Lord included having the right relationship with my family, and not using "my ministry" as an excuse to neglect them. It was no longer "my ministry." It became "His ministry through me." That is what the Scripture is talking about in Psalm 127:1: *"Except the Lord build the house, they labour in vain that build it: except the Lord keep the city, the watchman waketh but in vain."*

And as an added bonus, it became "our family's ministry" and I mean that literally. My gymnastic daughter was one of the strongest workers in our church, and she still is. Both daughters brought more people to church and to the Lord almost by accident than their mother and I did on purpose. How they did it would take another whole story.

The Priority of a Minister's Family

"But if any provide not for his own, and specially for those of his own house, he hath denied the faith, and is worse than an infidel" (1 Tim 5:8).

What do you think of when you read this verse? What are the things we need to provide for our families? A good living? A safe home life? Enough food of the right kind? Good education? All the latest gadgets and fashions?

Paul's encouragement to ministers in 1 Timothy 5:8 it is not just about material things. There are things more important such as spending time, teaching, talking, loving, showing how important they are to the parent. It is keeping promises and protecting them from the many dangerous things in the world. It is showing you care about them. It can even be tough love, letting them suffer the consequences of their actions, and then showing them unconditional love, and helping them not to make the same mistake again.

What about just spending time with them? That, of course, depends on what you do with your time with them! If the time is spent criticizing and complaining about something, then it is counterproductive. I have found that the thing that most people need is just someone to listen sincerely and honestly to what they have to say, without judging, criticizing, or making a joke out of it or using it against them. They need someone who can listen with unconditional love, no matter what they look like or act like; no matter the assets, liabilities or handicaps. It is sometimes better just to pray with them and help them to see how you love them.

Conflicts can be caused by not understanding what God really wants from us. We can have ideas of what our family ought to do that are not from God. When we expect them to understand that something comes before they do, they should not and will not understand. If it is the work you do, other people, your reputation, or anything but the Lord Himself, then that causes conflict. Go back and look at your expectations of them and what is the source of those expectations.

Just because you were raised a certain way does not make it the right way. I was raised in a home where the natural volume was loud, louder, and loudest. No one ever considered that shouting was anything but normal. My wife came from a home where a voice was never raised in anger or anything else. We both had to adjust and understand that our way was not the only way, or even the right way.

There is no way you can keep your children from making poor decisions and choices. But you can be there and help them get through those difficult times. You can set an example in the way you handle adversity, in the way you follow the Lord and put Him first in your life.

All this cannot be done if you spend all your time trying to buy them with material things. Remember, if you did not have a family, you would still work at a job. They are not the only reason you work. Show them how important they are to you.

In our family, our children knew they came before anyone or anything else, except God. We tried to show them this in many ways. I can remember several times church members came to me or my wife and complained about something one of our daughters had done. My answer was always the same, "Really? She did that? She probably learned it from your kids." We never expected them to be perfect. I never told them they had to be or do anything because I was the pastor or missionary. That would make it about me, about my reputation, about my standing in our community. I never told them they could not do something because we are Christians, that implies that if you are not a Christian it is okay. I always said, "We don't do that because it is wrong!"

If you do not put your family in the right place in your priories, you could lose them or hurt them. We have all seen the heartache that brings to ministers and their family. God established the home and the family before He did anything else. It should have the first place just after our relationship with Him.

What is a home? When you say "home" what are you thinking of? One's place of residence: a domicile, a house, habitat? The social unit formed by a family living together? A familiar or usual setting or the focus of one's domestic attention? Home is where the heart is? A place of origin?

I remember hearing a story about a little girl who was staying in a motel with her family and she was asked by a lady why they were there. She explained that they had just moved from another city and did not have a place to live yet. "Oh, the lady said, you don't have home yet?" "No," said the little girl, "We have a home, we are just looking for a house to put it in."

I want to share with you a Valentine my daughter sent to me and her Mother several years ago:

A Special Valentine Message for Both of You

As I have thought about our home, and the home Otto and I are building now, I have come to the conclusion that 'home' is not a place, a house, a city, or even a group of people who live together.

I think that 'home' is the essence of relationships built over years, bound up in memories, and stored in the heart.

When I think of home, I don't think of a place, which is good because if I thought of one place, I would be leaving out a lot of other places where we have lived and grown. I don't think of a particular house, or even of a particular city.

I think of specific times and specific feelings. Special events, hugs, sermons, fun, and love.

Defining home as a place would rule out all the times I visit home each day. You are home to me... and I visit you often every day.

I think of what I think you would say about some particular thing I'm working on, or involved in, or looking at. I hear your voices and carry on conversations with you. In a real way you are my conscience, my companions, my confidants.

Because of you I see things twice; I see them the way you would, and then the way I do. Sunsets are beautiful to me because they have always been beautiful to you... a book is doubly good as I imagine the enjoyment you would be having as I read along.

When I eat a good meal, I wish you were there to enjoy it with me.

When I hurt, I am comforted by the fact that You would do anything to keep me from hurting if only you could... even if you never know that I'm hurting, the awareness that you would comfort me if you could comforts me!

There are times when you chastise me, and give me advice.

I lay in bed in the morning and I debate whether to get up and fix Otto breakfast, and wafting through the air I hear you, mother, "Get up and fix your wonderful Otto a good breakfast... be a good wife!"

When I'm tempted to compromise and not do my best, I hear you, Daddy, saying, "Do your best, you know we'll be proud."

I feel your love, and your confidence every time I try something new.

I think twice before doing something wrong because of you.

I'm not saying that there aren't times when I long to feel a real physical hug... sometimes I wish we were all back under the same roof.

Sometimes I wish 1 could just fly home and be a little girl again whose greatest worry was trying to stay awake until her daddy came home so she was sure he was safe.

Sometimes... but most of the time I am thrilled to have the home you deposited in my heart to visit.

Home must be a place we carry in our hearts. It must be! Otherwise I would be homesick, distraught, insecure and alone.

Thank you for the home you have given, for the home you maintain; for the sense of security that our home provides even when it's clear around the world.

***

She and her family are halfway around the world in Central Asia. But we are closer than some parents who live in the same city as their children.

Sam Keller, is a semi-retired BBFI missionary with 35 years in Australia. He also pastored in USA; started four churches, two in USA, two in Australia. He and his wife, Karen, have two daughters and six grandsons, all active in the Lord's work.

STAY

Jerry Burton

I WAS DRIVING into my new town for the first time to assume the pastorate of my first church, and the question went through my mind, "I wonder how long I will be here?" I preached my first sermon as pastor on December 15, 1979. My final sermon was Christmas Day, December 25, 2011. I completed 32 years as pastor of this great church.

I asked myself on several occasions, "Is my staying here a matter of stability or insanity?" The ultimate answer to the question of staying, in my heart and mind, was this: "This is the will of God for me at this time in my life", and that lasted for 32 years in one place. The pastor who preceded me was there for 3 years. He resigned on a Sunday morning, told the congregation that "Ichabod" was written over the door of the church and it would never amount to anything, and he never came back. Two months later I became the pastor and faced a group of people who were totally beaten down.

In addition to this issue, there were five different factions in the church, each with a different concept of how the church should be run. Not only that, but financially the church was in very poor condition, so much so that when I came to candidate, in order for me to stay in the local motel, the church had to prepay the bill. One more thing: After I had been pastor for five years, I walked into one of the local restaurants to get a cup of coffee. I sat down beside a very successful businessman in town whom I knew. He leaned over and said to me, "You're in!" I said, "What does that mean?" He said, "We were watching to see if you would stay, and you did. You're in."

Did I ever WANT to leave? The answer is yes. Did I ever TRY to leave? The answer is yes. But God ... that is the answer to both issues.

Now, SINCE I stayed, was there any value in that? Does longevity have any real benefits, or is it that one just doesn't have the opportunity to go anywhere else? Here are some of the benefits of longevity in the same pastorate, as I see them.

The Church Profits Greatly

When I came, the church was deeply in debt. We owned two buildings; a Christian school in one, and our offerings were scarcely enough to meet weekly expenses, much less do anything extra. Over the course of time, God allowed us to close the school (there was another Christian school in the area), sell the school building, and completely renovate our existing buildings so that they were maintenance-free externally and beautiful on the inside.

In addition, we were able to raise the monthly support of the missionaries we were supporting and also add a substantial number of missionaries to our missionary family. As pastor, I was able to make several trips to various mission fields, because the church could financially afford to send me and my wife.

In addition to paying off our debts, we were able to save the money needed to renovate our buildings without having to take a bank loan. The bank WANTED to loan us money, but we did not want or need to borrow money.

The Community Becomes Your Family

I was seated in my office one afternoon and the phone rang. When I answered, my personal physician said, "Jerry, this is _____. I was just in the ER at the hospital and there is a man there who is dying. I told him he needed to get his house in order. I wonder if you would mind going by to see him?"

My doctor was a practicing Catholic. I went immediately to the hospital to see the man. He was indeed dying and I was able to lead him to the Lord before he died. I tell you that story to illustrate the value of longevity in a community and the way the community becomes your family.

I became involved in the Chamber of Commerce and also one of the local service clubs (Rotary). These two connections gave me access to the business leaders in our town. These connections led to my being able to provide counseling to several of the leaders when they were in need of some help, either with their marriage or other family issues. The superintendent of schools in our city was a member of my church. When an issue came up that concerned me or some parents in the community, I was able to go to him directly and talk through it.

You have probably already figured out that I pastored in a rather small community. Some think this is all the more reason to not stay a long time. After all, you run out of prospects pretty soon! Right? Think about this. When people are looking for help, they go back to the last source of help they can remember. In a small community, you are able to saturate that community frequently with the gospel and information about your church. You then often become the last source of help they remember.

Longevity Forces You to Study the Word

If a pastor stays at a church for 4 or 5 years and then moves on to another place, chances are he will simply go back and rework those 4 or 5 years of sermons and preach them again. You say, "What's wrong with that?" Nothing. But when you stay in one place for an extended period of time, you cannot just go back and pull out an old sermon and hope no one remembers.

I had one lady in my church who wrote the date in her Bible when I preached from a passage. And she would remind me if I used the same passage again. I told her it was the same verse but a totally new message. So, for me, longevity forced me to be a continual student of the Word. I spoke four times a week and tried to always have something fresh and relevant. During the summer months, I gave the congregation the opportunity to suggest Bible questions they wanted answered or topics they wanted me to speak about. That gave them some input and gave me an awareness of their needs.

Longevity Builds the Families in Your Church

Your families grow accustomed to your preaching and teaching style. Some will love it and will stay with you. Some will say, "You can't preach a lick" and leave for what they think are greener pastures. Those who stay will grow along with you. You will see the children grown to be adults. You may even have the opportunity to marry some of them. You get to be involved in the birth of their children. You are called upon to bury their parents and grandparents.

When tragedy and hard times come into your life, your church families will watch you to see if you practice what you preached. They will learn from the way you handle tragedy and heartache. After I had been pastoring for about 25 years, my wife developed cancer, lived just eight months and passed away. As you can imagine, I was emotionally crushed. I took a few weeks off from preaching to clear my head. When I came back to church and preached that first Sunday, someone said to me, "Pastor, you showed us a lot. You showed us how to handle loss in our lives. Thank you." They will never know how much that meant to me. But I believe that what the Lord used to teach me, He also used to teach them through me.

Longevity Allows God To Do What You Could Never Do On Your Own

My entire tenure as pastor in that church was a learning experience for me. On my last day there, I was learning how to turn over the reins of the pastorate to another man. I wanted them to see him as their pastor and not still be looking to me for answers and I told them that. Thankfully, they did not call me to answer their questions. They went to their PASTOR.

Everything that was accomplished was not because I was accomplished or experienced or smarter than anyone else. The truth is, even though I had previously been a staff member for 19 years, I had never been in a place where the buck stopped with me. If one comes to the pastorate after several years serving as a staff member, in whatever capacity, the pastorate is NOT the same. Every decision you make affects more than just you. It is now your responsibility to consider the whole of the ministry, not just your particular arena. I had to learn to pastor everything from the janitor's closet all the way to the top.

When you realize that a church is a family, every time a pastor leaves is like a father leaving his family. The next man coming in will be a step dad until he gains the confidence of the people. We all know that families have members who do strange things. Church families have the same characteristics. Leaving because you have an issue with a family member may simply be Satan's way of rendering the church ineffective, because if one family can cause pastoral turnover on an ongoing basis, Satan wins. At some point, someone must become the leader the church needs in order for the church to have the impact on its community that God intended. Maybe that someone is you.

Staying is not always the easiest decision to make, but sometimes it is the best decision to make – for you, for the church, for the community, and for the kingdom of God. Make certain that what you choose to do is what God wants and not simply an easy out because of a momentary difficult situation. Remember, when in doubt, don't!

Jerry Burton is a retired pastor, now living in Lima, OH. He is married to Carol Burton. Jerry is a graduate of Baptist Bible College, Springfield, MO, Luther Rice Seminary with an MA and MDiv., and a graduate of Louisiana Baptist University with a PhD in Biblical Studies. He taught for Moody Bible Institute Evening School for 21 years.

Avoid and Overcome Discouragement and Depression

Jim Baize

CHRISTIAN MINISTRY HAS been my life for the last 50+ years. I received Jesus Christ as my personal Savior as an eight-year-old boy. My spiritual life did not progress quickly after that because we moved from the church and community where I trusted Christ to another community without a strong Gospel church.

About eight years after my salvation, a new Baptist church began meeting in our town. My mom and I attended, thought that was where God would have us to be, and stayed there for the next few years. Shortly after high school, in my second year of college, I would surrender to the call of God on my life at that church. That next fall, I attended Baptist Bible College in Springfield, Missouri, in preparation for a life of ministry. I graduated from BBC and entered fulltime vocational ministry in 1970 as a youth pastor.

Full time Christian ministry should not be considered a profession – it is a calling. No one should enter the ministry just because they think it might be a good job! A pastor should be God-called. And the callings of God are without repentance; that is, when God calls us, He doesn't later change His mind! (Romans 11:29) It is God's plan for us to enter a life of service to Him and to others, and to remain in that role until He calls us out of this world. (I point out this difference between the ministry being a job and a calling because not understanding that distinction may, itself, contribute to mounting frustrations and discouragements. If we endeavor to do something that we were not made for, no matter how "good" it is, there will be a lot of pressures and problems that result.) When we surrender to a call, we are saying, "This is what I will do with my life." And that ought to be what we do from that point on. God-called ministry is for a lifetime.

So, is that what actually happens? In too many cases, the answer is a resounding "NO!" In no time at all we learn that ministry is not devoid of valleys, attacks, and the enemy. It took no longer than about a week for my wife and I to realize that ministry was not a "safe house" insulating us from discouragement. Too many pastors enter the ministry with the idea that all will be sweetness and honey. Ministry is messy. People's lives are not perfect. The more people to whom you minister, the more messiness one encounters. I certainly don't want to discourage anyone with this statement, but I do want you to engage in the ministry to which God calls you with eyes wide open. I want to be real about our expectations so we won't be taken by surprise.

Ideally, we ought to enter the ministry for the long haul, but, as I mentioned, that does not always happen. I recently made a study of pastors who remained in ministry long term. I consulted some well-known authors and what they had to say about ministers staying in the ministry. Here are some books and articles I found helpful:

1. *10 Pieces of Pastoral Advice*, Thom Rainer

1. *Dangerous Calling*, David Tripp

2. *Don't Do Stupid*, Thom Rainer

3. *8 Keys to a Lasting Legacy*, Thom Rainer

4. *How to Last in Ministry*, Rick Warren

5. *It Takes 5-7 Years to Become the Pastor*, Thom Rainer, www.thomrainer.com

6. *7 Symptoms of Those Who Do Not Finish Well*, Thom Rainer, www.thomrainer.com

7. *Stupid Things Pastors Do to Mess Up Their Ministries*, Thom Rainer, www.thomrainer.com

8. *10 Pieces of Advice Pastors Have Trouble Receiving*, Thom Rainer, www.thomrainer.com

9. *3 Reasons Pastors Drop Out*, Caleb Kolstad, www.the-cripplegate.com

10. *Finish Strong*, by Steve Farrar

This is just the tip of the iceberg! Pastors are quitting ministry in droves according to many who follow the trends. (Most studies cite somewhere between 1,500-1,700 pastors leave the ministry a year!) Why are they quitting? There are some unusual pressures on pastors. Among them, discouragement – or even worse, depression – takes a huge toll.

Steve Farrar's book, *Finishing Strong*, postulates that only one of every ten trained full-time ministers will still be in ministry after thirty years! Some of the causes for discouragement or depression are: the conflicts, complaining, and murmuring of church members; a lack of fruit and spiritual maturity in members; the apathy of members; the members who leave the church for "no particular reason," the high expectations of the members; being expected to perform tasks for which the pastor was not formally trained; too many meetings and committees; family concerns; staff issues; and a lack of volunteers. Wow! That is quite a list and I am sure it is not complete!

All of these components result in a pastor feeling lonely or like a failure, which can lead to spiritual or moral failure. (Our enemy knows when to attack!) A wise pastor will safeguard himself against these things as best he can.

If depression is such a spiritually fatal affliction (and it can be), what can one do about avoiding it? I learned early on that there are times no one else can help us get through those valleys. There are times when one's wife or friends are not readily available. What can we do in those times to avoid the pitfalls of discouragement?

A young man named David taught me a valuable lesson in this regard. His instructions are found in 1 Samuel 30. In this narrative, we find David and his men returning home from the battlefield. As they approached their home base – a town named Ziklag – they noticed something very unusual. There was a stillness that disturbed them. When they got closer, they saw smoke rising through the tree line where their homes were located. They quickened their pace. As they got to the camp, their worst fears were realized – Ziklag had been raided and burned to the ground. All of their family members and possessions had been taken!

Verse 4 describes the returning band's initial reactions: *"Then David and the people who were with him raised their voices and wept until they had no more strength to weep."* Have you ever been there? Have you ever wept until there were no more tears? Have you ever faced a situation that seemed beyond your control, leaving you helpless, sad, defeated, and discouraged? Of course you have. (If you haven't, you shall very soon!) No one gets away with living without having disappointments and discouragements. Some of them are small, even trivial. But others are life-shattering. This was a life-shattering and life-altering event in the lives of David and his men.

Pastors are people, too. We have life-shattering events that take place in our personal lives just like everyone else; but, in addition, we help shoulder the cares of a congregation. The losses our members suffer also take a toll on us, their pastor, with each ensuing crisis. I honestly believe that when a church family loses a member in death, part of us dies with them. Our tears are every bit as salty and genuine as are the blood family's. David grieved alongside his men. He grieved for his own loss, and he grieved for his men's loss. I know that because that is what good leaders do!

David's own family was taken hostage, his goods stolen, and his house burned to the ground. He had lost everything just as his men had. But he was saddled with an additional burden – his men blamed him and spoke of stoning him to death in verse 6!

They were so broken they had to find someone to blame. David was their leader, so this must be his fault, somehow.

Encourage Yourself in the Lord

The secret that David taught me concerning how to overcome discouragement and, therefore, depression begins to unfold, in verse 6. *"But David encouraged himself in the Lord his God."* The New King James Version says, *"But David strengthened himself in the Lord his God."* The Hebrew word translated encouraged in the KJV and strengthened in the NKJV means "to strengthen, prevail, harden, be strong, become strong, be courageous, be firm, grow firm, or to be resolute."

I imagine David beginning to talk to himself: "Hang in there David. Don't give up, boy. God is still in control. Remember, He helped you with the lion and the bear. Oh, and don't forget Goliath! It's going to be OK, David. Keep on keeping on! This, too, shall pass. All things work together for the good..." Maybe those weren't his actual words, but somehow, he mustered the courage he needed to overcome this devastating time in his life. He realized that this was not the end. There was something else that could still be done. When we run out of things we can do, God is just getting started. Nothing is impossible with God. When we are at the end of our rope, we can tie a knot and hang on by encouraging and strengthening ourself in the Lord.

Inquire of the Lord

He didn't stop with just encouraging himself in the Lord. In verse 8 David *"inquires of the Lord, saying, 'Shall I pursue this troop? Shall I overtake them?'"* In other words, he prayed.

He sought the Lord. He asked God what he should do. Instead of focusing on the discouragement at hand, he sought a plan of action. "God, what do You want me to do about this?" Bible commentators note that if David had asked God about his actions that led up to Ziklag being sacked, maybe this whole trial would never have happened. He was originally motivated by the fear of Saul, who was seeking his life, to go join up with the Philistines in battle against Israel! The Bible doesn't say he prayed about that questionable decision. Often times we get ourselves in certain situations that seem hopeless because of our prior actions. If we would pray more before every decision, perhaps we could avoid some of the discouragements of life that can lead to depression. Nonetheless, now David prays to God for further instructions.

Pursue

David got his answer from God. *"Pursue, for you shall surely overtake them and without fail recover all"* (v. 8b). It is one thing to know what God wants us to do. It is another to actually do it. In this case David got his marching orders (literally) and acted immediately. *"So David went, he and the six hundred men who were with him, and came to the Brook Besor where those stayed behind, who were so weary that they could not cross the Brook Besor"* (v. 9).

As an aside, this brook was a stream of water in the southern part of Judah that emptied into the Mediterranean Sea. Would you like to know what the name Besor means? It means "cheerful!" It is almost as if God is saying to David, "Take heart... cheer up...I've got this now!" When God begins to lift our heavy burdens, when we realize we are not alone, when we once again have hope – the clouds begin to lift and we can smile again! Note, the battle wasn't won yet; their families were still help captive, but God was working! Whatever situation we face that discourages us begins to dissipate after we have encouraged ourselves in the Lord, sought His will, and followed His plan for our lives.

Recover All

What follows next in the text is a story within a story. Verses 11-16 tell of David's finding a young Egyptian who had been left for dead by the raiding Amalekite band. He had been with the Amalekites when they attacked Ziklag. He promises to lead David and his men to the Amalekite camp as long as David protects him and doesn't return him to his slave master. David assures him he is safe and the Egyptian leads David to the Amalekites, who are celebrating their victory with food, dance, and wine. It was happy hour for the Amalekites! That all ended with David and his men descending upon the enemy, swords drawn, showing no mercy.

This part of the story ends with the enemy defeated and David's men having recovered all – all their family members who had been kidnapped; all of their possessions that had been taken – everything was recovered and the Amalekite raiding party was either killed or on the run! With all this done, they return to the Brook "Cheerful" and divvy up the recovered property AND the spoils of war retrieved from the Amalekites. Now they were even better off (financially) than they were before the raid on Ziklag. They recovered ALL of the captives, ALL of their possessions, and now, in addition, they had the Amalekites' spoils of war!

I can't tell you how many times David's formula has taken me through a dark valley. Many times I have: 1) encouraged myself in the Lord, 2) inquired of the Lord, 3) pursued, and 4) recovered all! When one repeats this cycle often enough, they tend to not let things get them down initially as much. God has delivered them so many times before, they know He will do so again! That gives us HOPE! Hope makes us smile in the face of difficulties. And that is how we can win over discouragement and depression. This is one of the most valuable lessons I have learned in the ministry.

Jim Baize was saved at First Baptist Church of Chicago Heights, IL, in 1956. He accepted the call to ministry and graduated from Baptist Bible College in Springfield, MO in 1970. In 1973 he became lead pastor of Midway Baptist Church (now called Ocean View Church) in San Diego, CA and served there until 2015. He became lead pastor at First Baptist Church of Coronado (CA) in 2016 and serves there currently. Pastor Baize and his wife, Pat, have three children, two sons-in-law, one daughter-in-law, and three grandchildren.

HANDLE DIFFICULT CRITICISM FROM MEMBERS WITH WISDOM

Dale Peterson

O F A PASTOR'S several difficulties, one of the most difficult is receiving personal criticism. While some well-meaning souls may offer clichés such as, "A pastor must have a tough hide but a tender heart," let's face it — personal criticism can hurt.

Further, the hurt of criticism is exacerbated by the fact that pastors are (or should be) limited in the number of people with whom they share their personal feelings. We certainly do not want to be guilty of carrying problems home, burdening spouses, or negatively influencing our children. Seldom are we willing to vent to colleagues in ministry, lest they think poorly of us.

So, what can we do aside from feeling trapped in the lonely, private bubble to which pastors often default? Beyond taking "the burden to the Lord and leaving it there," are there steps we can take to minimize the damage that criticism can do emotionally? Can we help others while addressing and alleviating the criticism? Is it possible to use this process to help grow the congregants — at least those involved in the issue?

Parenthetically, many of life's difficulties may be dealt with by asking three simple questions. First, what is the problem? Second, what is the solution? Finally, how can I enlist your cooperation in solving the problem? These three points will unfold as you continue reading the chapter. (Names and locations have been changed to protect both the innocent and the guilty!)

It came unexpectedly — seemingly out of nowhere — ambushed. There was little doubt the barrage of criticism was planned and coordinated in advance of that Monday night deacons' meeting. Although there were no rounds from sniper rifles penetrating me, each critical comment tore into my mind. I was in the crosshairs of at least four men seated around the conference table. It took a few minutes to sink into my mind that I was pinned down by the crossfire.

I had been invited by a large percentage of the congregation to become the pastor of First Church. For both congregation and pastor, a new era had begun almost two years earlier, though no one knew what that would look like over time. Perhaps no one ever does. That's life!

Sadly, at times there can be church members — and it's seldom very many — who do not "get their way" in a congregational vote and refuse to be team players. While a majority move ahead under the new leadership, a few may quietly resent that the congregation did not move in the direction the minority had hoped. This became apparent at First Church while I was under fire in that Monday evening meeting.

During the first two years, many good things had been happening. A good number of people had been converted, accompanied by subsequent baptisms. This always brings a measure of excitement to a church. New visitors were attending almost every week, and a healthy percentage of them chose to attend the new members' classes and joined the church.

While good things were happening outwardly, a sinister force was working covertly. Since my focus as pastor was on the good things that were happening, I was somewhat oblivious to rumblings beneath the surface.

However, during this monthly deacons' meeting, a floodgate of criticism erupted. It soon became apparent that at least four of the seven-man board had quite a list of things that were wrong with me as the pastor. From what they were saying, most of the congregation felt the way the deacons were describing.

Fortunately, I had the presence of mind to take good notes and generally keep my mouth shut, asking an occasional question relative to whatever was being leveled against me at the moment. I sensed that was not the time to be defensive, so I listened carefully and took notes.

LESSON: *Listen carefully and patiently and take good notes*

Those notes later became a vital part of the "game plan" that I assembled after seeking counsel from a wiser and older pastor.

LESSON: *Seek wise counsel from others who have survived*

By the time the clock chimed midnight, much criticism had been leveled. The chairman acknowledged that they wanted to give me time to respond, and indeed, I would need to respond. But I stated that, while I would like to do so, I didn't want to do so at such a late hour.

When I suggested reconvening at 7 p.m. Tuesday, one of the men said, "Oh, pastor, I know you would like to have time to pray over these issues. We can certainly come back tomorrow evening." Frankly, I had not even thought of praying over their criticisms! I just wanted to get out of the building before killing someone!

LESSON: *Allow yourself time to process what has been said.*

Another man spoke up to say that he couldn't meet the next night because he had a dinner appointment. I calmly swung into action, choosing my words carefully.

"Gentlemen, if I understand what you have been saying to me this evening, these issues are very serious and are very important to you. If these things are accurate, we dare not delay in addressing them, so I will see all of you here tomorrow night at 7. I will be prepared to address your comments at that time," I concluded.

If you're still reading, and you are a pastor of any length of time, you know how these things can affect us. I was angry. I was discouraged. I felt like quitting. I wanted to lash out verbally.

I did not sleep very well that night. (Does any of that sound familiar?)

By now, you're wondering, "Well, Dale, how did you handle the situation?" I'm glad you are wondering, because we'll now walk through the important steps that I was able to navigate.

After an opening prayer by the chairman of the board the next night, the deacons turned to me. I'm not sure what they were expecting — perhaps that I would be so demoralized that I would resign or perhaps that I would be defensive. If so, they were disappointed. Let me walk you through some critical steps.

First, I thanked them for their forthrightness and honesty with me about their feelings and thoughts. "That must have been difficult to sit here around the conference table and say these things to your pastor, so I thank you for your candor," I stated, all the while looking into each man's eyes.

LESSON: *In everything, give thanks.*

Second, I outlined for them the "game plan" that I wanted to follow. This proved to be a vital step in both giving them every benefit of doubt and ensuring that I had heard and understood clearly what they had said to me the night before. It would also become a teaching tool in problem-solving for each of us.

Here are the steps that we used.

Item by item and using my notes from the previous night, I repeated to them in my own words what I had heard them say and asked if I had heard them correctly. We didn't move to the next item until it was clear that we mutually "understood" what each "problem" was. We barely made it onto page two of my legal pad of notes by 10 p.m. Tuesday! After ensuring that we would resume thirty minutes after Wednesday night ministries ended, we adjourned.

After an opening prayer about 8:15 p.m. Wednesday, the chairman stated that he didn't feel that it was necessary to dredge up every detail. Now, it was time for firm leadership and measured bluntness. Without wavering, I spoke slowly and softly while looking intently into the eyes of the men.

"Gentlemen, you have just told me that you haven't a clue about how to solve a problem. You were the ones who brought these issues to the table, but you have a pastor who does know how to solve problems, and we will solve each one of them."

Without missing a beat, I resumed where we had left off the previous evening. We would finish this phase and the remaining two pages of criticisms late Friday evening. The men were exhausted, as was I; but we were going to address each of their concerns — whether real or contrived. No one brought up the notion of abbreviating the process.

LESSON: *Develop a solid game plan and stand your ground graciously.*

After taking a break Saturday and Sunday nights, we resumed meeting on Monday evening. In this meeting, we returned to the beginning of their list of criticisms and discussed specifically what it would take to resolve each problem they had originally brought to the table. Further, we discussed each possible solution until we reached unanimity concerning what action (presumably on my part) would be required to resolve each problem.

By Wednesday night of the second week, I fended off a few feeble attempts by a couple of the men to modify and shorten the process, but I refused. Surely they were wondering by now what kind of Pandora's box they had opened! However, by week's end, we had completed the second step. Although I was beyond weary after two weeks of nightly meetings, I found some warped delight in watching them leave each night like whipped pups with their tails tucked between their legs!

LESSON: *Endure hardness as good soldiers. Some battles take time.*

After the problem-solving stage, week three brought us to another step that caused the real critics on the board to again resist. In this step, we would return to each item and attach names to each issue, so that I knew with whom I was dealing and with whom I needed to resolve the problems. If the critics had humored me with the first two steps, they certainly balked at this one! One deacon protested, "These are our friends, and they have taken us into their confidence!"

Once again, I leaned forward, placing my arms on the conference table, I explained myself and confronted the fallacy that they knew anything at all about solving problems in a spiritual manner and in a spiritual environment. With as few words as possible, I staked out my claim.

"Gentlemen, once again you confirm your lack of understanding of the situation at hand and how to solve the issues. These may very well be your friends, but they are the sheep of a pasture for which you are trying to hold me accountable. You have exposed yourselves as either being dishonest or lacking an understanding of how all of this works.

"We are going to attach names to each issue so that I can apply the remedies that you have agreed would solve each problem. If you are unwilling to name names, then I am left to assume that you are the one who has the problem."

Believe me, the room was quiet! I glanced at my notes. Thankfully, with each item and a few statements about each, I had also written the name of the board member who had brought the issue to the table. I quickly continued.

"So, John, if you are unwilling to tell me who I have offended by (here I named the supposed offense), you leave me no recourse than to believe that you have the problem with me and you have been unwilling to be honest about it."

Deathly silence. Four red faces. Eight eyes looking down at the table. But I noticed a twinkle of hope in three pairs of eyes before I returned to the process of naming names. We wrapped up this phase by 9 pm Thursday night, and I suggested that Friday's meeting should only take a few minutes.

LESSON: *Ministry is primarily about people – and that can get messy sometimes.*

After opening prayer at 7 p.m. Friday, I produced for the men paperwork reflecting open times that I had available to go to visit the people with whom I had (or supposedly had) issues. I asked each board member to sign up for a couple of times that they could accompany me. I did not reveal which members we would visit. (My intention was to take with me the board member who had brought an issue to the table and visit in the home of the John Doe who had the problem. I wanted to ensure that true feelings were being expressed by both deacons and members alike — and in my presence.)

Visitation was begun, but the first home visit was a setup! Although the board chairman and I were to make the visit, the parties involved had decided to have another board member present as well. Although this was the very first visit, little by little, a few board members revealed themselves as being dishonest and manipulative.

LESSON: *Not everyone is honest, even in ministry. Let the dishonest reveal themselves; you be honest in everything.*

The visit was intense. Rather than staying on point to do and say what the board had agreed upon, I was now being verbally attacked by a husband, his wife, and two deacons! The more intense they became, the more gently and softly I spoke.

Having exhausted their supply of criticisms of my leadership, my preaching style, and all the new people taking over, the couple had run out of words, and I could speak. Looking them in the eyes, and glancing into the deacons' eyes, I let them know what the deacons and I had agreed to over fifteen nights of meetings. Looking intently at the two deacons, I said,

"Tonight (Deacon #1) had agreed to come here with me to (and I inserted our stated purpose and solution). However, by (Deacon #2)'s presence here this evening, they have shown themselves to be dishonest men and all that has been accomplished here is four professing Christians attacking their pastor relentlessly — a pastor who came to resolve a conflict."

I abruptly prayed what was, I would like to think, a gracious prayer, said "Amen," and stood to my feet. Turning to (Deacon #1), I asked, "Would you like to ride back to the church with me or would you prefer to have (Deacon #2) take you to your vehicle? Surprisingly, he said he would ride back with me, which he did — in silence.

Upon returning to drop off (Deacon #1), I put my Tahoe into Park, turned in my seat to face my passenger. Calmly and softly, I began and confronted him with his dishonesty on several situations that he had orchestrated. He was unfazed by any of it — no remorse whatsoever!

LESSON: *By their fruits you will know them. Not everyone who cries, Lord, Lord--*

As a reader, you would be bored to tears if I regaled you with story after story as the follow-up visits continued. Thankfully, the subsequent home visits were not as intense or dramatic as the first one, but each visit confirmed in some manner that taking personal and patient responsibility for resolving conflicts in a church is always the proper course for a pastor.

Through the years, I've noticed that my own defensiveness has subsided. I find less reason to argue or debate. Once church members have steeped themselves in gossip and criticism, they seldom repent and never do so when confronted by a defensive clergyman.

LESSON: *Don't feel compelled to "keep score." There is One in Heaven who does that.*

Dale Peterson is president of Gospel Alive, Inc., a Michigan-based 501(c)3 organization focused on global evangelism and discipleship, and a former pastor of thirty-plus years. Dale and his wife, Debbie, reside in Clarkston, Michigan. Chapter used by permission. All Rights Reserved.

CARE FOR THE DEAD AND DYING

William VanValkenburg

S HE HAD RED hair, her face was covered with freckles, and she had a grin that spread from ear to ear. Judy was my first girlfriend. She died after battling leukemia while we were both students in the same fourth-grade class. I and another young boy were selected by our classmates to choose flowers for her funeral. I can remember climbing into the back seat of our teacher's blue Chevrolet and going to a local florist to choose flowers. We decided on pink roses.

Two days later, the members of our class walked solemnly to the local funeral home down the street to pay our respects. Her parents greeted us at the door and led us into a large room where Judy was laying in a small white casket. Our pink roses were prominently displayed on a stand near the head of her casket. It was a difficult experience. My ten-year-old heart was broken and my mind was filled so many questions.

And there were others including both of my grandfathers but it was not until my own father was unexpectedly killed in a car accident that the reality and profundity of death really hit home.

My father had worked in the same factory in Adrian, Michigan for almost thirty years. He claimed that he worked in the factory to support his dairy farming "hobby." He was driving home after work that fateful day just as he had done hundreds of times before. But everything changed that Thursday afternoon in May of 1975. A drunk driver crossed over the center line (in a "no passing" zone) in order to pass a semi truck that was apparently traveling too slow. To avoid hitting him, my father drove into the ditch, swung back onto the roadway and hit another car head-on. The motor of the small car my father was driving ended up in the front seat and my father ended up in the back deck.

My mother, two sisters, and I were devastated. Not only did we have to deal with the shock of losing my dad so suddenly and unexpectedly, but there was also the trauma of having to deal with making funeral arrangements followed by the task of having to slowly piece our lives back together in the weeks and months that followed. I've never been the same.

As I look back upon that tragedy that occurred over forty years ago, I can see how God has used that experience to enhance my ministry, especially when it comes to ministering to the family of a deceased individual as well as those going through the dying process. I can remember attending a Pastor's Conference many years ago and during one of our informal times of sharing, a number of the pastors admitted that ministering to the dying and having the responsibility of conducting a funeral service was their least-favorite aspect of their pastoral ministry. This was stunning news to me. God selects certain individuals to become pastor-shepherds of His sheep and how important it is that those pastor-shepherds lead their flock confidently throughout their days and especially through those times when life is coming to a close.

The statistic has remained the same since the days of Adam and Eve — one out of every one person will die. Someday. Somehow. Somewhere. God has determined that our time on earth is limited. The Holy Spirit impressed upon the writer of the New Testament book of Hebrews that *"And inasmuch as it is appointed for men to die once and after this comes judgment."* *(Hebrews 9:28 NASB)*

The word "appointed" is an interesting word, isn't it? The New Living Translation puts it this way "And just as each person is destined to die once and after that comes judgment." It's really quite simple — God knows just exactly how many days you and I will enjoy life on this earth He created, and when those predetermined days are over — so are we. The Psalmist says this *"As for the days of our life, they contain seventy years, or if due to strength eighty years...(Psalm 90:10 KJV)* so *"Teach us to number our days that we may present to You a heart of wisdom (Psalm 90:12 KJV).* Some of us living in America do live into their 70s, but many do not. I believe the point the Psalmist is making is that life is unpredictable, and temporary, and it's important that we each make the most of each day God gives us. Each day is a gift.

It's one of the most poignant scenes recorded in all the Scriptures. After pronouncing a specific blessing for each of his sons and including a prophesy concerning each of their futures the writer of Genesis says *"When Jacob finished charging his sons, he drew his feet into the bed and breathed his last, and was gathered to his people." (Genesis 49:33 NASB)* We then read in Genesis 50 of the process of embalming, observing the appropriate days of mourning, and of Jacob's eventual burial in the land of Machpelah. It's a powerful scene, filled with emotion and human drama.

Situations similar to the patriarch Jacob's final days are re-played daily all around the world and wise is the pastor who has learned how to minister with compassion and tenderness to individuals and families as they journey with their parishioners through *"the valley of the shadow of death." (Psalm 23:4 NASB)*

I did some research recently in which I perused a number of Christian College catalogs. What I discovered is that when future pastors are trained in our Bible College and Seminaries, they spend semesters learning proper skills in hermeneutics and preaching techniques (and rightly so), they are taught effective methods of counseling those with a variety of needs, they are challenged with the importance of reaching the lost, and yet in most cases, little attention is given in how to minister effectively to those individuals in the dying process, the families that surround them, and how to conduct an appropriate and meaningful memorial service.

Throughout my last forty or so years of pastoral ministry, I have conducted hundreds of funeral services. Those services range in size from a small service of just four people (including the funeral director and myself) to an auditorium containing hun-dreds of mourners. Just a couple of months ago, I conducted three funeral services in one week — for a 101-year-old, a still-born baby, and a 31-year-old who died tragically of an apparent heroin overdose. Last week I had two services, one for a man who had been estranged from his children for over thirty years, and the other for an individual who had become so depressed and despondent they they ended their own life. I have conducted services for three different generations of the same family (at different times, of course). Every service is unique because every person is unique. I am convinced that there is never a time when a pastor should pull out his little black "Minister's Service Manual," write in the name of a deceased person in the blank spaces and consider doing that as an acceptable and meaningful memorial service.

Because of my interest in helping others minister effectively to those in the dying process as well as families going through a time of grief and loss, I was invited a number of years ago to teach a two-hour evening class on the subject at the former Tyndale Bible College near Detroit. My fear of teaching a class in Bible College was totally unfounded as it was truly a delightful experience. Before I began my presentation, I encouraged the students as I was speaking to write down any questions they might have with the promise that I'd try to answer those questions, if possible, at the conclusion of class-time. I was greatly surprised at the response of the students and the depth of the questions they asked. In fact, the response was so positive the professor invited me to return the following week to speak to the students again. Students asked questions like: "What happens when someone dies?" "Why does God allow Christians to go through pain and suffering?" "Are funeral services really necessary?" "What does the Bible say about cremation?" "What do you say to someone who knows they are dying and are afraid?" "What do you say to family members?" "Why does God allow children and teenagers to die? Those were all excellent questions and we spent another two hours discussing these many important issues.

Conducting a Meaningful Memorial Service

One of the questions asked most frequently by those students had to do with why do we even have funeral services and what should be included. I would like to address some of what I think are the do's and don'ts of conducting meaningful and appropriate memorial services.

I can't ever remember a time when I did not feel "called" to preach. I was raised on a dairy farm. As a teenager, I would sometimes walk into our barnyard, climb on top of a huge rock, and preach hellfire and brimstone sermons to our herd of Holstein cows. They responded by producing pure buttermilk when it came to milking time. I graduated from Bible College in June of 1972 and entered a full-time Christian ministry of reaching children and teenagers for Christ in the local schools. What a wonderful privilege of being able to lead hundreds of boys and girls and young people to faith in Jesus Christ. My phone rang in October of 1972 and upon answering I heard the news that a dear man I had come to know as "Grandpa Bernie" had died suddenly of a massive heart attack. I was asked to conduct his funeral service. It would be my first. To the best of my knowledge, this kind and gentle man had never walked through the doors of a church, had never read a Bible, and had, most importantly, never received the gift of salvation.

What Did I Do?

I knew I needed help and so I called the pastor of the church that I had attended throughout my teenage years. The advice he gave me was invaluable and I have followed that advice throughout the hundreds of funeral services I have conducted since. His advice to me was two-fold: (1) make the funeral service personal, and (2) share Truth.

Make the Funeral Service Personal

I have the privilege of conducting between 40 to 50 funeral services every year. And, yes, it is a privilege to be asked to minister to a family during a time of loss. In every case, I make an appointment to meet with the family of the deceased preferably the day before the service. Because I have been a part-time staff member of a local funeral home for the last fifteen years and longer, I am frequently called upon to conduct a service for an individual that I did not know personally.

When I meet with a family, I ask a lot of questions. Generally I have in front of me an obituary written by the funeral home staff to use as a guide so my goal in meeting with the family is to learn more about the individual than what is contained in the obituary. What was this person's history? What were his/her likes and strengths? Did he/she have any hobbies, etc., and I always close our discussion by asking the question "Using just one or two words how would you best describe your loved one?" You would be surprised at the amount of information I can learn in just a few minutes of talking with the family members.

Now I'm sure someone reading this will ask "what if it's impossible to meet with the family?" In situations like that, I'm forced to ask questions via a phone conversation. In a recent situation, however, even that was impossible. The various family members were all driving from a great distance, the service was scheduled for quite early in the morning making it impossible for me to meet with anyone or even have a conversation. So at the beginning of the service I simply asked the family members (whom I had just met) if they would permit me to conduct a rather informal memorial service. They agreed and so I began by asking them a questions about their loved one and as they responded I asked another question and when the service was done many of those family members came to me with tears in their eyes saying it was the most personal and meaningful service they'd ever been a part of.

Let me ask you — doesn't the deceased person that you've been called upon to conduct a memorial service for deserve to have their life-story reviewed? I used to have a sign in my office at church that read something like "everyone has a reason why they act the way they do — discover the reason." I have modified that statement by reasoning "everyone has a story to tell about their life — discover their story." The owner/director of the funeral home where I am employed reminded me recently that a funeral service is for the benefit of the family... of the living. It's the primary means of helping them to recall good memories which will, in turn, encourage healing and relief from their grief in days to come.

What I Will Not Do

There are a few things that I will not do in conducting a memorial service. Ever.

First, I will not lie. I remember listening to a pastor doing an eulogy for a man a few years ago and as he spoke I was tempted to get up and go peer into the casket to see if he was talking about the same individual we had placed in the casket. Along with that, I've learned that sometimes the least said, the better. If the individual had not lived an exemplary life, the memorial service is not the place to "hang out someone's dirty laundry."

The second thing I will not do is preach anyone into heaven. In EVERY service that I have conducted, without fail the loved ones of the deceased will make comments like "he's so much better off now," or "she's finally free of all her pain and suffering." Many times I find myself thinking — "Well, no." Without Christ (if he didn't appear to be a believer), he's not better off now, and no without Christ (if she didn't act like a genuine Christ-follower) her pain and suffering has actually just begun. Just remember — you are not in a position of being able to determine who's gone to heaven and who hasn't, so be very careful about what you say and how you say it.

Something else I will not do is publicly condemn an individual's lifestyle. For example, a few years ago a local pastor was called upon by the family to conduct the funeral service for a young man who died a slow, horrible death after contracting AIDS. The family had already been devastated because their son and brother had chosen an ungodly and unbiblical lifestyle, and they did not need to hear the rantings of the pastor as he condemned homosexuals and sent them all to hell. I sat there listening with an increasingly heavy heart because this pastor so added to all the pain and turmoil this family had endured for many years.

During the service for the individual who had died of an apparent heroin overdose, I had a choice to make. This person was a very kind and generous individual but had struggled with addiction for most of their life. My challenge to those who gathered for that very difficult memorial service was to not let this person's addiction define their life. They deserved better/more than that.

What is Truth?

The Scriptures make it very, very clear that there is an eternity in heaven to gain and an eternity in hell to shun. I've always found it interesting that Jesus talked more about hell than He did heaven and I believe He did that because He wanted so desperately to keep every man, woman, and young person out of that horrible, eternal place of torment and suffering. We are created as eternal beings. The writer of Ecclesiastes makes it clear that… *"He has also placed eternity in the human heart." (Ecclesiastes 3:11 NIV).* You can disagree with me if you'd like, but I do not believe that the funeral service is the place to unload one's knowledge of hell upon those assembled.

There is one particular pastor that, boastfully realizing he has a captive audience, preaches a sermon on hellfire and brimstone as part of every funeral service he conducts. Please don't misunderstand what I'm writing here. Do I believe hell is real? Absolutely. Do I teach and preach that those who die without putting their faith and trust in Jesus Christ will spend eternity in pain and suffering? Again, absolutely. But there is a time and place for such instruction and it's not during a funeral service.

I believe that, instead, it is important to share the Gospel in a clear and simple manner. I frequently base my funeral message on what is undoubtably the best known verse in all the Bible, John 3:16, or I use the very familiar Romans Road to Salvation. And there are certainly many other Bible verses and passages that can be used appropriately.

Memorial Service for a Believer

What a wonderful joy it is to have the opportunity of sharing the life story of a man or woman who has walked with God through the years. When I'm presented with such an opportunity, I frequently refer to those comforting verses in John 14 concerning our "going home" and, in the case of a female, I often focus on the qualities of a "worthy woman" as found in Proverbs 31 and close by highlighting how *"a woman who fears the Lord, she shall be praised." (Proverbs 31:34 NASB)* And, of course, there is always a special joy involved if the individual is someone that you have had the privilege of leading to Christ and helping them grow in their walk with Him.

Teaching Your Parishioners

It's important as the pastor-shepherd of the flock God has entrusted to you to teach your congregation the importance of preparing for one's death. I once preached a six-week series on death and dying and on the last Sunday I handed out forms I had created on which each parishioner could write down their preferences on what they wanted done if they were to die.

Many of those parishioners, once they had their form filled out, sealed them in an envelope and brought them to the church office where they were placed securely in a file... ready to be opened if, and when, the time came. On this form, they were able to include songs or specific Scriptures they wanted used during their funeral. They were able to express their desires on where they preferred memorial donations be directed, who they would like to have serve as casket-bearers, etc. I have been told by a number of families of how thankful they were to have those forms to guide them in their decision making. You would be amazed at the number of families that walk into the funeral home to make final arrangements that are clueless as to what their loved one would have wanted.

Most funeral homes also have a trained pre-need counselor on staff. These individuals are willing to work with individuals in determining their desires and to get them in writing. Many people chose to pre-pay their funeral expenses while other chose to simply make the decisions on funeral arrangements and have their funeral home of choice keep them on file. I've found it beneficial through the years to have a trained pre-need counselor attend a small group of church members, especially a senior citizen group, to give an informative and detailed presentation.

I have heard many people complain about the costs of funerals, and yes, they are expensive. But let me ask you something — have you had any surgery or medical procedure done lately? Because of a broken knee I was forced to have surgery in the spring of 2018. I was in the hospital for just three days yet the bill totaled well over $100,000. I've never been so thankful for insurance in all my life! Think about it. The funeral home has to pay for someone to retrieve the body from the place of death, has to pay the salaries for a variety of staff members (run the office, help park cars, work during a visitation), has to buy supplies, maintain equipment including a number of vehicles, keep facilities maintained, pay for utilities, spend time making arrangements with those who will be involved in a service as well as with cemeteries and vault companies, etc. Remember, too, that much of what a funeral home does is mandated by the laws of the state, county and the cemetery involved, meaning, there are many expenses the funeral home has no control over.

Church Growth Because of Funerals???

I was privileged to pastor a rural, country church for almost thirty years. Not many men are able to enjoy the privilege of such a long tenure in one location. During my years of ministry there were a significant number of individuals and families that became active members of the congregation primarily as a result of my ministry to them during a time of crises and/or death. Because I had ministered to them in what I had hoped would be a kind and compassionate manner, they made the decision to begin attending church services. They then heard the Gospel preached repeatedly, they responded by giving their lives to Christ, followed Him into the waters of Christian baptism, and continued in maturing as a dedicated Christ-follower.

Ministry of Presence

When I first began in pastoral ministry, one of my biggest fears was that of going into a home where a death had just occurred. I just never knew quite what to say or how to say it. Do I share some Scripture with the family? Do I pray with them? I eventually learned that, yes, it's important to do both of those things, but the most important and meaningful aspect of my ministry was simply being there. It's what I call the "Ministry of Presence." Not necessarily saying anything. Just being there. Holding hands. Wiping tears. Sharing memories. When a family has recently lost a loved one, they're not looking for advice or various opinions their pastor might have concerning a funeral service, etc. They simply want to know that you are there and that you care.

A Final Note of Caution

Let me challenge you that are involved in Christian ministry to never make conducting a funeral service primarily about earning a few extra bucks or adding to your savings account. I'll never forget the new pastor who arrived in town after serving a congregation in a larger, metropolitan city. After being handed an honorarium for conducting a service for a member of the parish, this pastor looked at the funeral director and asked "What is this? The amount of this check is nowhere near what I'm used to being paid and if you can't do better than this in the future please don't call on me to conduct any more services in your funeral home." The funeral director was speechless and, as a fellow pastor, I felt embarrassed. Conducting a funeral is all about ministry NOT about generating income. If you get handed an honorarium (as you will in most cases), consider it a blessing, accept it with a thankful spirit, and move on.

We all need hope in our lives. Families going through a time of bereavement are seeking hope. As ministers of the Gospel, we are to be hope-givers. If you have viewed conducting memorial services as a more negative aspect of your ministry, ask the Lord to help change your attitude. Look at a funeral service as a means of getting to know one of your congregants better or as an opportunity for learning someone's story for the very first time. You have been given the awesome privilege of recalling that person's life-story and sharing Truth.

Bill Van Valkenburg currently serves as Pastor-On-Staff at the Anderson - Marry Funeral Homes (Michigan). He has over forty-five years of pastoral experience, with thirty of them in the same church. Bill and his wife Rosalyn have been lifelong residents of Lenawee County in Michigan.

Made in the USA
Middletown, DE
07 September 2019